ANATOMY OF A CRIME

ANATOMY OF A CRIME

TOM SMITH

CHAPTER 1

The realization that time, the ultimate thief, had snatched most of my life and locked it away in a memory bank hit me hard. A fruitless journey littered with squandered opportunities and futile social activities; happiness was always transient and ever elusive; tranquillity an alien concept - a privilege I rarely encountered. Choosing the right path proved beyond my capabilities, choices invariably paved with physical and psychological traumas. Placing faith in fellow human beings often came at a price and embracing the charlatans became my specialty.

Fat Sid, a glib tongued manipulator who had the ability to make money and attract those gullible enough to listen to his tales of criminal escapades, was the most devious of all the crooks and cheats that littered the paths I trod.

Sid was in his late twenties when I had the misfortune to meet up with him. He was the proprietor of a down-market sleazy nightclub located in the backstreets close to Liverpool town centre. Physically he resembled a Chinese Buddha; his large bovine head was straddled with spaghetti-like strands of hair in a futile attempt to disguise his premature baldness. His belly protruded over his trousers as if he had a sack of potatoes stuffed inside them; he wore expensive Italian leather shoes; his face was baggy and pale; his chin was moulded onto his saggy neck like a stack of pancakes and two piggy eyes continual flickered as he observed everything and everyone around him. His Quasimodo-like appearance belied a man with an extremely sharp but totally corrupt and immoral brain. Sid was in the business of making money and self-preservation, whatever the cost, as I and legions of others were to discover in the whirligig of time.

After frequenting this seedy all-night dive and indulging in a few cursory conversations and establishing a cordial rapport, Sid eventually propositioned me. He suggested that it would be mutually beneficial if I had a meeting with colleagues of his, who I had heard were engaged in heavy but lucrative robberies. This smooth-talking, reptile-tongued imposter persuaded me with tales of vast sums of money that had been obtained by the group of robbers that he looked after. I took the bait to my eternal regret, the nettle of greed had been grasped and the consequences of that fateful night have haunted and tormented me ever since.

"This is Billy and this is his brother Vinnie," Fat Sid barked as he introduced me to the pair of robbers.

"OK mate. Heard good things about yer," I retorted as we exchanged handshakes.

Billy and Vinnie had a reputation amongst the criminal fraternity as two game and capable armed robbers. They were reputed to have been responsible for several major crimes that netted them large amounts of cash. They were early thirtyish, powerfully built and physically fit, dressed in designer clothes, five ten in height and well groomed. Could be mistaken for a couple of successful entrepreneurs.

"Grafting with anyone?" Vinnie enquired.

I paused before replying. All eyes locked in on my lips.

"No no. I was doing a bit with some north-enders, nothing too heavy. Fuckin' missed more than we got," I said, indicating that I was up for business with them and their mentor Fat Sid.

This discussion was taking place in a local park. The rendezvous was arranged by Sid. We strolled around for a while exchanging gossip about individuals that were familiar to all of us. Guys that were in the jailhouse, how long they were entombed for, who put them inside, the infidelity of their spouses and girlfriends. The conversation cut to the chase; I was invited to participate in a future armed operation.

I let the greed factor override my hitherto rule of only discussing this type of criminal activity with the principals who were to actually taking part in the crime itself. I realised that Fatso physically wouldn't be able to carry out an active role in an armed assault, consequently his presence raised a seed of doubt in my mind. The primeval sixth sense of survival that is innate in most criminals bounced around my frontal lobes telling me that there was something not right about this fat businessman. I ignored the signals and put it down to paranoia, a paranoia that had developed during a long spell in the urinals of the English penal system. I remember this moment as if it were frozen in time. Sid's demeanour and profile reminded me of a predatory shark as he chipped in with grandiose plans of how he could invest the proceeds of the robberies. Building property portfolios and buying into the licensing trade. He boasted about the corrupt council officials he had in his pocket which enabled him to purchase chunks of property way below market price. What he never disclosed was his close ties with a high-ranking police officer. This piece of intelligence was not detected until decades later.

"I will legitimize the money and make you millionaires. You'll become men of property," he boasted, smiling greedily as he nodded his head and gripped our shoulders as if we were a group of comrades about to celebrate a victory.

The social formalities complete, a further appointment was arranged between the brothers and myself to plot an attack upon a postal sorting office. Vinnie broke away from the other two and beckoned me towards him.

"Listen mate, this is the way forward, fuck blowing your dough on birds and booze. Let it work for you. Sid's connected;

he's set up companies, there's bent briefs on the firm. He fronts everything and we will be able to sit back and draw wages," Vinnie proclaimed emphatically.

"It sounds the business. I'm game - let's see what happens down the line," I replied as I shook his hand and departed in the opposite direction.

Hindsight is a wonderful thing. Vinnie was completely under the spell of Fat Sid's persona; he was mesmerised by his verbal dexterity and his knowledge of legitimate business affairs. He sensed my apprehension and used the promise of financial security to allay any doubts that I nurtured. In retrospect I should have volunteered to help clear the Cambodian minefields.

Alas, I was ensnared by greed and wanton need. I drove away musing over the proposition and the very real possibility that I could earn a substantial amount of cash and also get involved in a legal business enterprise. I found this appealing and decided to commit myself to the project. It never crossed my mind that things could go wrong and I could end up in a jailhouse. My sense of survival had been nullified by Sid and Vinnie's tapestry of wealth and the good life.

The gullibility I had in my mental locker at this time causes me acute embarrassment whenever I cast my mind back to this particular phase of my journey. I would probably have invested my capital in the future of the Yorkshire coalfields.

During this period the inhabitants of my genetic pool were outlaws. Crime was the common denominator. Money the motivator. Prison an occupational hazard that was accepted by most - but not all. Rumours sprouted up that certain criminal groups were trading with the authorities. Instead of a prison sentence for their transgressions they would walk free on a technicality. The usual excuse was that they had corrupted police officials, paying them various sums of money according to the gravity of the charges levelled against them. Coincidentally, associates of these criminal Houdinis would simultaneously be arrested for past misdemeanours and packed off to jailhouses.

Circumstantial evidence indicated that these experts on technicalities had cooperated with the authorities, pawning their comrades so that they would avoid a prison sentence. They hid behind an edifice of geniality, which masked their treacherous black hearts. They truly ran with the hares and the hounds. Exposure was extremely rare. They became important and valued assets of the constabulary. Scenarios were created to protect their identities as they progressed to become successful undercover agents and an integral part in the police's stance against crime.

I was never privy to this knowledge nor would I have given too much credence to it at the time. Informants were shunned like pariahs to be abused and scorned. A stigma that branded the sinner and the sinner's family. This climate, in tandem with a certain naivety made us cannon fodder for the undercover crews that polluted the criminal labyrinths.

This was the embryonic stage of Sid's crime syndicate; he needed to boost his capital influx in order to fulfil his empire-building aspirations. His grasping sausage fingerprints stained the entire spectrum of crime: Drugs, fraud, robberies, false documentation and IDs, forgery, a multitude of rackets - if it made money Sid was involved.

The next few weeks I got into the swing of things, reconnaissance missions of the target, stealing the appropriate vehicles, acquiring weapons, escape routes, back up plans, who does what.

From our observations we concluded that Sunday night would be the ideal time to strike. We had observed that the time-lock on the vault was released at one a.m.; the money was then removed by postal workers who began stacking it inside pigeonholes in a security cage. Each individual pigeonhole represented the cash amount for a post office. Our calculations put the total amount at five-hundred-thousand sterling (£5million at today's rate).

Under the cover of darkness, we would climb onto the roof of the postal sorting office and observe the activity and functioning of the skeleton crew who worked the early-morning nightshift. The routine was noted as was the location of the bandit alarm - nothing sophisticated, just a screamer that had to be struck manually by a postal worker. Satisfied that logistically everything was in place, we prepared ourselves for this piece of work. We arranged to reconvene one more time prior to embarking on the graft.

CHAPTER 2

A lady I was romantically involved with at this time had an uncanny gift of assessing the psychological profiles of people according to their horoscopes. She never forgot a person's horoscope and on most occasions her analysis proved to be correct.

Relaxing in her house, stretched out on a sofa, she commenced to read aloud my horoscope. I've never believed in this mumbo-jumbo; it ranks alongside voodoo, the occult and witchcraft as far as I'm concerned. This event took place two days prior to the robbery. I must add that she never had any inclination that I was involved in heavy crime and had no idea regarding the intended business at Worcester. She proclaimed, "Sunday will be an unlucky day for you, stay at home, something unpleasant is looming and will have a profound effect upon your life." I do remember reacting rather aggressively to this prediction and that I ridiculed her for harbouring such pagan beliefs. Years later she reminded me of the incident.

Sunday, the day of the robbery, I made arrangements to be picked up by Vinnie at 7 pm. We would drive to a lockup garage and take possession of the ringer and weapons - he duly arrived on time. Billy and two other plotters were to rendezvous with us at a pre-arranged destination with us from where we would debark for the Worcester project.

Inside the car with Vinnie, we headed for the meeting point when he announced that he was dropping in at Sid's house for a few minutes to clarify a couple of things. I thought to myself this guy's putting a lot of trust in Sid. A feeling of unease crept over me as he parked outside Sid's luxury detached house.

I waited in the car and wrestled with myself whether to abort this undertaking or not. My antenna was sending a surge of electricity down my spine, warning me that something wasn't right. The vibes were venomous; I expected to hear the rattling of a king cobra but instead my reverie was interrupted by the gruff tones of Sid's voice wailing to Vinnie that he'll see him in the smoke. Vinnie climbed into the car and we sped off. Another external alert that was ignored.

"What was all that about mate?" I asked Vinnie, as he weaved his way through the Sunday evening traffic.

Vinnie and his brother Billy had a capacity for violence, consequently they laboured under the misconception that Sid was intimidated by this latent capacity. They had an unqualified faith in Sid trusting him with their freedom and to a lesser extent, their lives.

"Don't worry about Sid mate, he's my man. I'm meetin' him in the Smoke after the graft. He's gonna invest a big chunk of the dough for us. He's fuckin' sound Tom." Vinnie replied emphatically as he probably sensed my overt discomfort regarding his diversion to meet up with Sid.

"Hope you're right. One fuckin' slip-up and we're fucked," I responded curtly. At this specific time in his life, Vinnie was a particularly shrewd operator and exuded confidence; I accepted his judgment.

I should have added the caveat that if this was my work, Sid would not have been privy to the imminent robbery nor the participants, even after the fact. We eventually met up with Billy on the car park of a tower block near the outskirts of Liverpool close to the motorway system.

It was a cold moonless night, a night to be sat in front of a warm fire not standing in a huddle running through the final details to ensure everything was in order. Satisfied, we hastily jumped into the motors and hit the road. We were like the early Viking marauders steaming through the counties hell-bent on plundering the wealth of the nation and alleviating the fiscal imbalances that existed between us and the ultra-affluent establishment.

Five conspirators set off in three cars, two plated up, stolen for the robbery plus one legal vehicle to be parked at a preselected position approximately a mile from the imminent building invasion. If successful, the proceeds of the crime would be transferred to the straight car and a designated driver, in this case Vinnie, would then proceed in a different direction to the remainder of us plotters. That was the plan.

At Hilton Park motorway services, Vinnie and I pulled in to top up with petrol. I was squatting in the passenger seat; suddenly my antenna picked up on a car stopping at an adjacent lane. I stared at the two occupants as one of them alighted and nervously fiddled about with the petrol pump. He and his colleague avoided eye contact, both were aged about thirty, both had the unmistakable aroma of active policemen, the vapours that drifted out of his mouth into the cold night air were uniform blue. I continued to stare at the fiddling, fumbling motorist as he went through the routine of filling up with petrol. Head down, he averted eye contact, looking into space, seeing nothing. Vinnie returned from paying for the petrol. I pointed out to him the possibility that the two guys were the Old Bill. He paused for a brief moment, swivelled his head, locked onto the suspect duo, he glared at them, taking in their demeanour and made an experienced appraisal of the situation.

"They look like a couple of fuckin' gays to me mate, The Old Bill would not be that fuckin' stupid to show themselves. Don't worry, your head's still in the jailhouse. The slippery pricks would not be so obvious," Vinnie declared, with the assurance of a man who had done it all before. I accepted this interpretation allowing Vinnie's streetwise survival instincts to dispel the fears conjured up by my psychic concerns.

"I hope you're right and they're not two fuckin' undercover shepherds," I retorted. Vinnie grinned and sallied forth.

Nevertheless, for the next half hour or so, we dawdled in the slow lane, our mental radar on red alert, seeking out signs of the two petrol pump gays. They had vanished. Content that these anti-surveillance tactics would have exposed any shadowing cops, we stepped on the gas and hastened to catch up with our cohorts on the road to Worcester.

The town centre was practically deserted as we weaved our way through the streets, eventually arriving in the darkness at a poorly lit industrial complex which was separated from the target by a railway embankment. We slowed considerably until a silhouette caught in the headlight waved; it was Billy - we flashed to acknowledge him, then cruised to a halt some fifty metres further on.

As we strolled back towards the rest of the crew, two couples stumbled out of a side street in front of us; the odour of cheap perfume penetrated my nostrils, one of the guys mumbled incoherently, a fusillade of laughter erupted from the group, we paused absorbing the moment as the quartet raucously departed in the opposite direction, the beat of stiletto heels mixed with a boozy jubilation began to fade as they staggered out of sight and out of earshot.

Billy cooed softly, his voice guiding us towards him in the blackness. We scampered off the road onto the embankment rejoining our comrades. A semicircle was formed around two large holdalls. Billy, ever the professional, a small torch gripped between his teeth, began dishing out the weapons and balaclavas.

I struggled into a boiler suit, placed the bally on top of my head, gloved up then turned to the brothers.

"You got the pump-action there," I enquired emphatically.

This was reference to a twelve-gauge, five shot repeater shotgun that had been loaned to mates of ours. Mates who employed the same methods of acquiring funds as ourselves.

"No. I waited all fuckin' night, they never showed. Fuck 'em. We can take this down with what we got 'ere," Billy stated affirmatively, brandishing a loaded magnum pistol.

This development created a modicum of friction and impacted on the strategy decided upon to accomplish the raid as swiftly and efficiently as possible. I had to intervene to prevent the duo coming to blows. Spontaneous tactics were employed. The original plan was a rapid assault on the security cage a blast in the air from the shotgun to stun and frighten the workers, apprehend them, control them, bundle them all together in the security cage, where they'd be securely bound and gagged. Thereupon allowing us ample time to steal the cash and make good our escape. We now agreed that I would head for the bandit alarm to the rear of the building, some thirty metres from the security cage armed with a pickaxe handle. The idea was to prevent any of the postal workers setting off the screamer that would probably thwart the attack. Everyone else would capture and secure a targeted worker.

Agreement reached, we clambered over the embankment and scaled onto the roof of the premises. We crept stealthily to a vantage point, a large skylight which gave us a panoramic view of the activity taking place below. Previous reconnaissance had revealed that four men manned the premises, one remained in the cage once the time-lock on the vault automatically deactivated, the other three busied themselves shifting mail bags, moving packages and sorting letters.

A window overlooking a corridor was jimmied enabling us to access a stairwell leading to the floor of the sorting office. Jay, who had covertly spied on the mechanics of the cash movements of these premises on three prior occasions, spotted a stocky male inside the security cage and declared he had not noticed him before.

"Count them," I said, moving closer to the skylight to scrutinize the characters below.

We both studied the movements below; it was like watching a stage play except this was for real. After a short while, content that only four people were visible, we crouched down in a corner to shelter from the cold night air, patiently awaiting the deactivation of the time-lock.

I remember Jay calling quietly that the lock was off and we immediately jumped up and crept towards the vantage point to verify the news. Inside the cage, red sacks which we knew contained bundles of cash, were being placed into pigeonholes within the cage.

"Ready chaps?" whispered Billy, as he checked the ammunition in the revolver.

"Let's do it," I declared, making a beeline to the jimmied window.

Silently, we clambered through the window and assembled at the head of the stairwell. I adjusted the balaclava so that my face was totally covered; the rest followed suit. We descended stealthily to the ground floor until we reached thick rubber revolving doors. We paused to peek through a plastic window located in the centre of the door; three workers lingered close to the cage, one unaccounted for. I whispered that he was probably in the aisles and that I would race to the rear to locate and capture him while they neutralised the others.

The internal layout of a postal sorting office resembles a library, row after row of three-meter high shelves encased in a large auditorium. A person in an aisle could pose a problem.

"Fuckin' go!" shouted Billy.

These three syllables have tormented me ever since.

They echoed the battle cries heard by those unfortunate souls about to meet their doom in countless conflicts across the ages. 'Lambs to the slaughter' is forever inscribed in my memory whenever I relive the incident.

I hurtled through the door, stave in hand, sprinting towards the bandit alarm, eyes peeled seeking the fourth worker scrutinising each aisle as I streaked passed. I paused briefly at the screamer shielding it with my body when I spotted the postal running towards a doorway and I gave chase. He shut the door after him which automatically locked, I crashed through and captured him.

He was hyperventilating and clearly in a state of panic. I calmed him down reassuring him that I had no intention of doing him any harm.

"Listen!" I said, "I'm going to take you to your mates and tie you up - nobody will get hurt. We're just going to take the cash, OK?"

He agreed to my demands. Grasping the collar of his coat, I proceeded to frog march him towards the security cage where I assumed the others had successfully concluded their part of the operation. I was about to enter an aisle when a masked figure yelled 'it's on fuckin' top,' and raced past me faster than a greyhound. Before I had time to compute or react to that fleeting vision, a large male wielding a scythe came steaming in my direction, baying like a lunatic. He wore a blue jumper, his hair was thick and bushy with grey clumps scattered about his head, eyeballs bulging almost out of their sockets. My initial thoughts were that this was a crazy have-a-go postman, consequently I shoved my captive to one side and tackled the baying nutcase. I avoided his clumsy swing and swiftly set about defeating and pacifying him. During the brief skirmish I inflicted damage to his arm and hand causing him to retreat whilst screaming,

"Get a gun down here, get a fuckin' gun down here."

I then realised we had major problems, something was drastically wrong. I attempted to pursue the scythe man, when I glimpsed Billy on his knees being beaten with a cosh. I sped in his direction, still thinking these were extremely brave postmen resisting our attempts to rob them. As I neared the bottom of the aisle my focus expanded taking in a disastrous chain of events that had transpired whilst I was capturing my selected quarry. There was a squad of armed police officers dancing around the prostrate bodies of the others and a marksman had a pistol pointing at Billy's head. I span round and made a run for it only to come face to face with the courageous constable Key, a fully qualified police marksman.

The officer had his arms outstretched in front of him, in a classic stance, a revolver gripped in his right hand; he was shaking uncontrollably as if he had been struck with ten thousand bolts of electricity. I stopped motionless, still gripping the wooden stave which hung loosely by my side. The intrepid constable's face was chalk white, his lips were trembling, I sensed the fear seeping out of his glands. "This idiot is going to shoot me" was instantly computed by my brain. I was about to utter for him to take it easy, when he opened fire, the first bullet shattered the bones in my left forearm causing me to pirouette backwards; the second shot hit my chest side on, bouncing off my sternum, deflecting off my collar bone before entering the lung. I was knocked off my feet. As I lay on the floor a large boot stood on my neck and a hand ripped the mask off my face; a gun was thrust against my temple and I could hear the hammer being cocked.

A voice bawled out, "He's not armed, leave him alone."

The voice pushed the would-be assassin off me. I recognised him; it was the postman I had captured. He undoubtedly saved my life.

Lying on the cold concrete floor with blood cascading from the wound to my arm and blood spilling out of the gunshot to my chest; in incredible pain compounding the dire straits I now found myself in, a vision of Fat Sid floated into my consciousness. "That bastard has pawned us." This thought amplified the agony as shock kicked in and the concept that I might die, alone, gunned down by law enforcers, blanked out the reality of this predicament - pain relief became the overriding priority.

The scythe man stooped down by my side, he lifted my head and placed a makeshift pillow under it speaking softly has he did so.

"I'm D.C.I. Fishwick. You're badly hurt. An ambulance will be here shortly."

An element of concern tinged the soft dulcet tones of his voice.

His right hand was wrapped in a white cloth stained with blood. I later discovered that he required a number of stitches; two fingers had been broken in the altercation between us. He bore no grudges and waited by my side until the paramedics arrived, flying in like Tasmanian devils. I lapsed into unconsciousness.

CHAPTER 3

Worcester Royal Hospital, a blurred face of a nurse is cutting off my clothes with scissors, a morphine drip is connected to my right arm, a medic is inquiring to what faith I belong, a doctor is shoving a syringe into my ribs. A priest sprang up from nowhere and began chanting a religious litany, fading in and out of my vision as he rambled on with his version of the 'resurrection shuffle'. Lucidity was replaced by a shroud of blackness. I was now in the hospital theatre where a team of doctors toiled ceaselessly through the night, battling to put me back together again - they succeeded.

I was kept sedated for a number of days in a medically induced coma. The most vivid memory I have of this episode is seeing myself in the operating theatre. I was ascending into a bright light at the apex of a cone shaped funnel, I was hovering in a vortex of brilliant whiteness watching a team of doctors dressed in green gowns, all had green caps; they were beavering away huddled in a circle. I identified myself quite clearly, an extremely weird and spiritual experience.

The surgeon heading the team that operated upon me explained the out-of-body vision to me. At one point they thought they had lost me but, because I possessed a strong constitution, the will to live, I survived the crisis and the umbilical cord of life rejected the magnetic pull of death and coaxed my soul back to kickstart my battered body. He explained it was a phenomenon that occurs when the heart stops beating in the theatre, many patients recount similar tales to mine.

When I eventually awoke to return to the land of the living, reality hit home like a smack on the jaw with a sledgehammer. A cop was seated in the corner, a gun protruding from a shoulder holster; my right hand was cuffed to an iron bed post, bandages swathed my chest, a drain dangling from my lung; my left arm was strapped across my midriff throbbing like a bad toothache. The vigilante cop was reading a comic, grinning like a gibbon, aware that I was awake. He uttered a few undecipherable words in a Brummy accent, pulled out a police radio and blurted coded gibberish into the mouthpiece. A few seconds later, in bounced a chief inspector, a toady hot on his heels clutching a briefcase in his hands. He shooed the Brummy out of the room and perching on the chair, he introduced himself.

"I'm Chief Inspector Pickles and this is Detective Sergeant Fishwick," he said with an air of pomposity and paused staring at me as if I were some kind of diabolical fiend.

I ignored the glare as his sidekick unclipped the briefcase and handed Pickles a file.

"Right," boomed Pickles, "you're in serious trouble, do you want to say anything before I charge you with armed robbery?"

I wanted to say, "who the fuck set me up" but it would be an exercise in futility; that data would be highly classified information and these two textbook cops would not be privy to such secrecy. I shook my head, keeping my thoughts to myself and said nothing. Pickles went through the formalities in a sing-song twang. Finished, he placed the charge sheet relating to the robbery on the bed. Fishwick, then interceded with a crude attempt to interrogate me.

"We have information and evidence that you were a conspirator in numerous other robberies, the modus operandi being identical to the Worcester robbery," he chanted like a monk's catamite, preening himself as he nodded to his boss for approval.

"Listen, Sherlock-fuckin' Holmes," I said, referring to Pickles, "you and Doctor Watson take your amateur detective bollocks out of here and come back when I have a brief present. I've nothing more to say to you. OK?"

I shut my eyes and totally ignored the verbal diatribe they hurled at me. After failing to engage me in a dialogue they shuffled to the door where Pickles fired a departing salvo.

"You're bang to rights you robbing bastard. Jail is where you're going for a long, long time," he stated vindictively. I expected Doctor Watson to poke his tongue at me. This occurred before interview-recording days when it was common practice for the law enforcers to verbal suspects up, usually putting falsified detailed confessions into the suspect's mouth. One particular police force had recently been exposed for a multi-paged confession they extracted from a deaf mute. They tried to justify this skulduggery by claiming that the officer who took the statement was an expert in sign language. A claim later refuted; it was discovered that the officer had difficulty signing his own name let alone deciphering sign language. Hence my reluctance to indulge in a bout of verbal swordplay with this pair of uninvited visitors. I now accepted my fate and thus adopted a philosophical approach – 'fuck it'. I drifted off into a narcotic fog; losing myself in the labyrinths of my mind, sleep a beautiful refuge. A hullabaloo disturbed this moment of tranquillity, a female's voice ranting at the comic reading cop. It was the brown-eyed clairvoyant who had predicted something bad was going to happen to me. She had driven down to visit me and seeing me cuffed to the bed had sent her into a rage.

"He's not a wild animal, the man's dying, Get them chains off him you evil bastards," she ranted dramatically at the cop who just sat there, annoyed to be disrupted from his crossword.

"I'm only obeying orders luv," he said feebly as he shrugged his shoulders. The clairvoyant had none of it, darting out of the room, bawling loudly seeking someone in authority.

Meanwhile the cop was blurting into his radio in a state of panic asking for advice. A short while later she returned with a senior doctor. He took a cursory glance at the cuffs tethering me to the bedpost and furiously ordered the cop to remove them that instant telling him that I was a critically ill patient and I was his responsibility. Trying to fudge the issue, the cop began stuttering and spluttering, waiting until he received the go-ahead on the phone. The doctor and the clairvoyant screamed abuse at him causing him to vault like a gymnast and unlock the cuffs.

"You fool! Your horoscope pointed out this fuckin' shit was gonna happen. Why didn't you listen to me?" she cried angrily, aware that I was now the property of the penal system for many years to come. There was no disputing her logic, a sightless retard would have picked up on the fact that something was seriously amiss and the incursion to rob Worcester should have been aborted. I deposited this truism deep within the graveyards of my mind. The die is cast - yesterday was gone. We conversed for a while arranging for a solicitor to contact the police to inform them that I was now legally represented and that any future interrogations would require his presence. This was a necessary precaution to deter verbal contamination. A few hours had elapsed when a superintendent marched in barking out orders into space, followed by two mongrel faced officers. Disregarding me, he instructs them to stay close to the bed. Two hospital porters scurried in and began pushing the bed out of the room. I was being transferred to the top floor as a security measure, the platoon of cops in tow. Cameras had been set up in the passageways with monitors placed in an adjacent room to mine. I began to speculate whether I had confessed to the assassination of J. F. K. or the Ripper murders whilst spinning through the twilight zone. The rural cops had taken paranoia to the extreme; little did I realize this was only the tip of the paranoia.

Rumour had it that they applied to the bomb squad to booby trap the roof and mine the fields at the rear of the hospital. They wept with frustration when the M.O.D. rejected their application. (Scouse Sarcasm).

My brother Kevin visited me; he was appalled at the extent of the police activity around the place. It was now a fortress with armed cops at the entrance, snipers on the roof, a helicopter in the sky and a full body search before being allowed to see me. Ashen faced, he asked me if I had started a war. I explained I was arrested and charged with a simple robbery but these soft bastards are making an epic film out of it, pointing at the cop who never left the room, eaves dropping on every conversation. Kevin shook his head in disbelief at the tactics employed to guard me, both of us were perplexed. I expected Steven Spielberg to pop up with a movie camera, surrealism prevailed. A consultant orthopaedist gave a disturbing prognosis about the trauma to my arm. The bullet had shattered the forearm bone requiring Kiel grafting, entailing bone from the hip being transplanted with a metal plate then Screwed into the undamaged bone. If this procedure failed the alternative was amputation. This news deflated me temporarily but positive thoughts muscled in allowing the consultant's words to be suppressed and buried in my subconscious. The punctured lung would heal, the bullet had been extracted and the prognosis was good.

After visiting the theatre to undergo surgery to remove a piece of shrapnel I awoke to a room full of cops, flapping like chattering chimpanzees. The pompous superintendent was barking out instructions, the gun-toting cops were bumping into each other in the close confines of the room. I was being transferred to a prison hospital. Apparently there was a tip-off warning the police that an attempt would be made by armed men to effect my escape from this hospital bed. These paranoid bumpkins had gone into 'Dads Army' mode; the

Superintendent assumed the mantle of captain Mannering, he was requesting air cover and motor cycle outriders whilst bullying and prodding the petrified unit.

"Positions Tango one? Positions Tango two?" he repeated incessantly as if he was repelling an invasion by an enemy force.

"Organization, there's no inter-service organization," he complained, looking to the heavens; the cops cowered and averted their eyes. Realising that this insanity was a precursor for a transfer to a jailhouse hospital, I fired a verbal volley at Mannering.

"Why don't you see if the Navy can spare a couple of gunboats or a submarine you fuckin' clown."

The comic reading cop burst out laughing hysterically; Mannering gave me a withering glance, then turned his attention to the laughing hyena.

"You incompetent nincompoop, Jones. Report for traffic duty tomorrow," he blurted out scathingly. Jones bowed his head sheepishly as the other officers smirked, relieved that they had eluded Mannering's tantrum. Police H.Q. alerted the gaggle of sleuths that all units were on standby, authorising the transfer of the subject to location WG1. This coded babble streamed out of Mannering's radio, audible to all within ten metres. On hearing the radio broadcast, I assumed WG1 referred to Winston Green Prison. I revealed this analysis to the audience sending a wave of frenzy amongst the officers. Mannering lambasted his crew of bumpkins for letting slip the intended destination of my imminent movement eventually focusing on Jones, who he threatened with disciplinary action. Jones protested his innocence pointing in my direction for support but I blanked his request and instead, I swore in disbelief at the incompetence of these elite enforcers as they behaved like a clutter of kids. They eventually shoved me on to a wheeled stretcher, shuttling me to a rear exit and into a waiting ambulance which sped off in a convoy of cars and motorbikes, sirens blaring, traffic stopped, helicopter overhead. Sheer madness. Have these rural sleuths mistaken me for a top Russian spy or international terrorist - a thought constantly bobbing about in my mind. The crime I had perpetrated didn't warrant this level of security. Later, I learnt that a section of the hospital was in the process of being refurbished. A large rubbish skip was on this section and according to an anonymous tip, the skip would be set alight as a diversion and a team of raiders would attempt to free me from custody. Absolute bollocks but I do know where this fraudulent information originated and the person responsible - Fatso. In a previous encounter with the Law, I'd been in police custody and the subject of an around-the-clock guard; complacency set in the mind-set of the guards and I took advantage of this and flew the coup making good my escape. This episode caused the Law acute embarrassment. Perhaps, I told myself, this previous episode contributed to the absurd, over-the-top actions of these rural cowboys.

Steamrolling up the motorway, the cavalcade of paranoid enforcers arrived at the foreboding concrete cesspit named H.M.P. Winston Green, a grim Victorian hellhole. I was booked in, and then carted directly to the prison's hospital wing where white smocked male prison officers welcomed me, parading under the guise of nurses. These guards were instructed to monitor my health, attend daily to my wounds, bath me and inject various narcotics into my veins whilst doubling as prison guards - a paradox in this violent environment. I was eventually lodged in a cell which masqueraded as a hospital room, adjacent to a ward, steel bars permitted a sliver of daylight to filter through a tiny window high up on a rear wall. A weather beaten cupboard rested against the head of the black metal bed, a white institutional plastic water jug perched atop the cupboard, graffiti adorned the pale yellow wall and the acrid stench of urine polluted the air. These were the standard features of these outdated, unsanitary human storage depots. A burly white-coated officer pranced into the cell bearing a tray of tea and biscuits. He introduced himself

"I'm Mr Wagstaffe. I'm the senior officer in charge of nursing. If you don't upset the boat we will all get along. You know you're a category 'A' inmate; certain restrictions will have to be imposed on you; a total segregation from other inmates, monitored visitors, a check on your whereabouts every twenty minutes and a low vision light will burn throughout the night. Behave yourself and the staff will do their best to get you well again. You can't get to the bell so, if you need anything, call out to the officer when he does a check on you."

He recited this monologue in a friendly broad Lancashire accent, sounding something like George Formby. As it turned out he was a rather decent sort of chap, an exception to the rule in this compost heap.

The weeks dragged by slowly; each day an exact replica of the next. I felt my strength returning and my breathing getting stronger; the main concern now was the traumatised arm. Visitors were restricted because of my category 'A' status. Each visitor had to be vetted by the police although whilst on remand, I was theoretically innocent and entitled to a visit and a quota of civilian food each day. This right was a source of continual squabbling as a succession of food-bearing friends were refused access after enduring hours of hostile checks or they would adopt a defensive position when strangers probed their bodies and private lives and were subsequently ejected off the plot.

Doctor Singh, a jailhouse quack, trotted into my cell accompanied by two male nurses. He wore a beige safari suit and gold rimmed glasses, had gleaming black pomaded hair that appeared to be glued to his scalp; his body was shaped like a boiled egg - aged about fifty and of Asian ethnicity. He stood there reading through my notes pausing to peek at me and emit an occasional mutter, acting out the role of a dedicated medical practitioner. Five minutes elapsed in silence, except for his superficial muttering when he handed the file to a nurse, whipped out a stethoscope, shimmied to my side, pressed the stethoscope to my chest, dawdled for a moment, mumbled, stepped back and then chirped out like a songbird,

"Why you're not dead is nothing short of a miracle. In my country the hangman would take care of thieves such as you." He spun and exited the cell delighted with his humane diagnosis; I let fly with a volley of abuse vilifying him as an imposter. This was the first of many run-ins with Dr. Singh the Bombay Duck. He was reluctant to prescribe analgesics to alleviate the persistent pain caused by my traumatised arm. His attitude was that the pain was a result of self-inflicted wounds stemming from my outlaw lifestyle. I had to petition the Home Office and communicate with my elected M.P. before Singh reluctantly relented, blaming the Screws for not following his instructions. The man would have fitted in with the ethos that prevailed within Nazi death camps. I dared question his medical qualifications one day, implying that the usual practice in Pakistan was that sons of the wealthy classes who struggled intellectually, were shipped off to the U.K. with bogus degrees, thus bluffing their way into the N.H.S. He began screeching like a banshee, bellowing in his native tongue, telling the male nurses to punish me.

"You filthy Englishman, you bloody thief, dirty convict. Indeed, indeed. Beat that man (pointing at me frantically) don't feed the pig." He lost control in front of the Screws who were mostly clandestine members of the National Front. He was lucky he was in the sanctuary of the penal structure otherwise his two body guards would be restraining him. Singh composed himself, stroked his grease ball scalp, then sauntered out of my cell. I was grinning at his antics and the Screw gave the thumbs up sign as he locked the door. The Duck's reaction to the innuendo I tossed at him boosted my waning spirits. Whenever the opportunity arose I taunted him, chipping in with snippets about arranged marriages if the son's sexuality was debatable. I suggested that the culprit was ostracised, either becoming a member of a religious sect or a doctor. He would fume...

"I'm no homosexual, you smelly English swine. In my country we would beat you. Indeed. Yes indeed beat you. Fornicating pig," he blurted out manically at the time of the gay innuendo. I would smirk with amusement each time Singh lost the plot. Mind games were an integral part of jailhouse culture it helped preserve one's sanity and repress the plague of penal boredom. One of the male nurses later told me that Singh had a deep abhorrence of me; he dreaded our encounters whereas I thoroughly relished the challenge and his obvious discomfort.

One morning a Screw tells me I'm off to an outside Hospital for an operation and whisks me to the reception area of the jailhouse. On arrival at reception, I was greeted by Mannering's task force of rural nutters who quickly shuffled me into a police van and drove out of the prison gates into a convoy of siren-blaring police vehicles. They reminded me of boys with toys, belting out phonetic guff into their radios as they terrified the life out of all normal road users. At the Birmingham Royal Hospital I was guided straight into the theatre and jabbed with a syringe which sent me soaring into dreamland. I opened my eyes to spot cops and Screws loitering about drinking coffee and discussing the latest episodes of the Muppet Show. Operation completed and arm plastered up to my bicep, a consultant orthopaedist stopped by to enlighten me, explaining that the

Kiel bone grafting was successful; a window inserted into the plaster-of-paris would enable him to address the tissue damage inflicted by the bullets exit. I expressed my sincere gratitude for his efforts prior to being rushed back to Dr. Singh's asylum. After a few more days under the auspices of the Duck and his nursing cronies I was deemed fit enough to be relocated into a prison wing.

CHAPTER 4

Approximately twelve hundred convicts were incarcerated inside the walls of this daunting institution at the time of my confinement (1980). Winston Green was a carbon copy of all the archaic jailhouses dotted across the UK with five wings, four stories high spiralling like spokes of a wheel from a command hub, the nerve centre of the prison. This is where the general prison population was housed. There was also an isolation unit, consisting of sixteen separate cells in an underground bunker. These specifically contained those unfortunate souls tagged as a security risk such as myself and my co-defendants. I was virtually entombed in the bowels of this urine-infested garbage dump which was to be my designated home for the next year or so, dependent on the trial date.

A quartet of huge beer-bellied warders greeted me on entering this gloomy control unit. Three of these hefty brutes wore caps with slashed peaks, the other was bareheaded, a fat-jowled mountain of lard. I knew by his white shirt that he was the senior officer in charge of the unit. The only thing missing from this band of merry men was the swastika armbands. The coercion commenced. Fat Jowls introduced himself.

"I'm S. O. Craig, this is my patch. Step out of line and we'll give you all the problems in the world. Comprehendez Smith?" he asserted puffing out his chest like a fighting bantam cock. The slashed-peaked trio glared menacingly at me in a show of unified intimidation. I disregarded his bullyboy attitude and locked eyeballs with him piercing his shallow edifice of bravado. I was not strong enough at this time for a confrontation with this gang of penal retards. I sighed deeply. "Ok boss, just show me my cell," I said tersely aware that Fat Jowl's fiefdom will be a test of my discipline and more significantly my spirits. These were hard-core thugs, brutes who clearly disliked all transgressors; they were hand-picked for an absence of passion and I assumed they had a capacity for meting out punishment. This attitude was at that time systemic throughout the penal colonies, condoned and sanctioned by successive governments as a means of controlling the inmate population. Campaigns by the quality press exposing such endemic thuggery eventually reformed the system and rid it of these chest-beating louts. However, this was in the future. Escorted to a cell, I noticed that several occupied locked cells were bearing the name-cards of my co-defendants. I called out their respective names and was met with a welcoming chorus of Scouse accents cheering my arrival and survival, banging on locked doors, creating a din. Fat Jowls bounced about delirious.

"Quiet you Scouse bastards. Lock that prick up," he roared belligerently, pointing a cosh at me. The slashed peaks shoved me forcibly into a rancid hole, slamming the door with hurricane force. The pandemonium drummed up by my mates carried on unabated, Fat Jowls was using his cosh to bash on doors threatening mayhem unless the noise subsided. I took stock of the situation. A tiny window almost level with the ceiling allowed a ray of light to filter in; a battered iron bedstead nestled against a paint-flaked wall; a cheap wooden table and chair were propped in one corner and opposite was a crude wash stand. A red plastic bowl sat in the middle of it and underneath was a filthy white plastic bucket for urinating in. That was it - my living quarters for the foreseeable future, bad enough without the added hassle of the Screws who would doubtlessly compound the misery, ensuring that the times ahead would be tough and uncompromising. Steel tipped boots stamping down on the concrete quadrant outside my cell, gradually increasing in volume, announced the arrival of the guards followed by a jangling of keys as the door was unlocked. A Screw chucked a bundle of blankets and two sheets onto the floor, followed by a dingy coloured towel. He stepped aside to allow another staff member pass who handed me a transistor radio and then requested that I sign for it. Before I had time to say anything the door was banged shut. Maybe they had taken a vow of silence to work in this subterranean cemetery or a policy of no fraternising with the animals. Pacing up and down like a caged bear; immersed in a round of mental gymnastics; a voice calling my name drifted through the window. I placed the chair beneath the barred opening, mounted it, and gripping the frame I answered the cry.

"Who's that?" I shouted out loudly, conscious it would be one of my co-accused. "It's me Billy. You Ok mate?" he retorted.

He was referring to my injuries not the scope of our predicament.

"A bit of a problem with the arm, otherwise I'm sound. Fuck 'em. What's this karsey like?" I responded, emphasising the last point.

"Tom, this is one fuckin' pisshole - the Screws are a shower of bullying tosspots. We're banged up for twenty-three hours and we're getting an hour's exercise on our fuckin' own. That's it. You won't believe the carryin' on of these bastards," he erupted vigorously, his anger obviously caused by The Jowl's liberty taking goons. Our brief conversation was interrupted by a Screw screaming at us to get away from the windows. We both told him to fuck off, the faceless complainer uttered some threats then retreated for reinforcements. It was sheer madness. The beat of boots clattering along the passageway, the jangling of keys, a rattling of locks, the door flew open, revealing a posse of heavy breathing goons, headed by the Fat Jowls. Cosh in hand, he stared at me menacingly.

"No bed for a week Smith. Disobeying an order, disrespecting an officer," he barked, smiling like a buffoon, ready for action. Two slashed-peak flunkies hustled in and snatched the bed like a couple of shoplifters before scampering back to the quadrant, Fat Jowls hovered by the door, a baboon smirk etched across his gob.

"Don't, I mean don't mess about with any of my staff. Down here I own you and your Scouse buddies. Ok?" he blurted as sweat dribbled down his blubbery cheeks.

"You big fat stupid lump of lard. Go and fuck yourself," I hollered, unperturbed at the abuse of power by this illiterate bully.

"Seven more days without a bed," he snarled, slamming the door shut.

The booming rhythm of the bouncing boots faded as the clowns marched back to their tea and tabloid crosswords. Billy endured a similar pantomime. Clowns they may be but dangerous loose cannons nevertheless. Rogue nightclub bouncers couldn't match the enthusiasm of this mob. I believe that if I hadn't been injured, Fat Jowls would have been a lot more forceful in his reaction to the lambasting I cast at him. I hadn't spent half a day in the unit and the boundaries had been declared; the mob were straining at the leash lusting for blood. An unsavoury atmosphere in which to contemplate the legal complexities coming our way. The regime operated like clockwork: 7.30 a.m. the cell main light switched on accompanied by speakers in the quadrant blasting out a song called 'Brown Girl In The Ring', by Boney M. The volume was deafening. This played for a full five minutes every morning, every day, week after week, month after month. It proved to be a catalyst for numerous outbursts of naked aggression by many inmates during my stay there. Even the most placid of men broke down after a prolonged spell of being woken up to the thunderous noise of Boney M. Three or four months into my stint, I was let out of my cell to slop out while the song was blasting out of the speakers. Enraged by this mental torture, I charged at the speakers tearing them off the wall and smashing them to pieces. The duo of officers looked aghast shoving me back into the cell. It cost me seven days no bed, and a fine. Next morning a new pair of speakers rocked away, playing that same old mind-bending tune. Breakfast served eight a.m. prompt, usually a ladle full of porridge, a postage stamp size portion of bacon, a mug of weak tea and four slices of bread. Once a week you got cornflakes and a boiled egg. All food was served on a metal tray which you ate alone in the confinement of your cell. Thirty minutes later the door would be unlocked to collect the tray. The routine was repeated at all mealtimes.

Other than the four charged with me, another four category 'A' prisoners were detained in this segregation unit; the remaining cells in the block were used as punishment cells to isolate offenders from the main jailhouse. The cell adjacent to mine housed Arthur Hossain, a notorious murderer. Arthur, along with his brother, had kidnapped and murdered the wife of the editor of the 'News Of The World'. He was nutty as a fruit cake; he always wore a bib and brace, slept in it, refused to take the thing off. Whenever the governor made his rounds checking on the 'A' which meant unlocking your door along with four bodyguards and asking if you had any complaints, Arthur would raise his arm and yell loudly 'Heil Hitler' the second his door was ajar. He never spoke to anybody in authority. I had a chess set in my cell, as did Arthur, we would often play of an evening shouting our chess moves out of the window. I heard Arthur was eventually declared insane which resulted in him being transferred to Broadmoor, an institution for the criminally insane. A couple of I.R.A. prisoners serving life sentences with a thirty-year minimum tariff were also caged in the unit when I arrived. They were subjected to special treatment from The Jowl and his gang of imbeciles which infuriated every other convict in the block.

Vinnie was unlocked at the same time as one of the Irish lads, engaged in a slopping out session, whereupon you use the toilet facilities and refilled water jugs. Fat Jowls refused to let the Irish lad top up with water, saying that he had been out of his cell long enough - five minutes. A squabble arose during which The Jowl and a slashed peak buddy drew their batons with evil intentions and moved towards the Irishman. Vinnie dashed to his aide confronting the thugs and challenging The Jowl to a fight. The sound of the dispute penetrated our cells causing an explosion of anger; the cell doors were smashed with chairs in a futile attempt to support our comrades. The Jowl backed down this time because, we assumed, it was suppertime and only a skeleton crew was on standby. I'm convinced if a full supplement of troops had been available blood would have flowed.

Vinnie was later charged with threatening behaviour and lost his bed for a month. Due to the fact that we were remand prisoners and interred in the jail's segregation unit, punishment was limited. A threatening behaviour allegation levelled against a convicted inmate would usually entail two to four weeks remission combined with a period of segregation and a good kicking. Remand prisoner status acted as a shield which discouraged the dogs of war from physical abuse as they were aware that a regular stream of family and solicitors checked on our well-being. Exercise time varied from day to day, however the one-hour period was a constant. A concrete square, twenty-five paces corner to corner, high steel fencing topped with razor wire, a miniature Stalag adjoining the unit provided a daily breath of uncontaminated air. I exercised with another prisoner, never a co-defendant, usually an I.R.A. captive. This pattern existed for each of us throughout our confinement. The law stated that if remanded in custody, the defendants should appear in court weekly until arraigned for trial. A date for trial followed committal proceedings at a magistrates' court wherein the Crown submits evidence to support a prima facie case against the accused. Captured red-handed, these proceedings in our case would be a formality, this assumption was generally accepted and expected. A trial date within six months was predicted by legal Cons.

The Worcester super-sleuths had other whimsical plans, which delayed the trial date by a year and a half. Holmes and Watson, in collusion with a multiplicity of police forces conjured up an all-embracing conspiracy charge. They adhered to a theory that if we had committed this crime then it was evident that we had perpetrated numerous others. The pair of sleuths trawled through lists of unsolved robberies over the past years to ultimately conclude we were responsible for five other raids on postal sorting offices. A truly preposterous allegation, based on nothing but their own inflated egos and the concept of modus operandi. Two of these postal raids occurred whilst I was in prison, something they failed to investigate in their haste to assign blame whilst confirming their status as bumbling bobbies. I was informed by a smug faced Screw that the police wanted to interview me - it was the intrepid double-act of Pickles and Fishwick. I insisted on a jailhouse officer being ever present if my solicitor failed to attend the appointment; this was a precautionary measure in the likelihood that I might be stitched up with verbal confessions. If not I would refuse to see them. My request was granted. Into the interrogation room swaggered Pickles with the chicken featured Fishwick two paces behind him. I was already seated and the Screw sat to my left. I had a sheet of foolscap paper and a pen on the table in front of me.

"You know why we're here?" Pickles rasped staring at the Screw and me, obviously annoyed at the Screws presence. They both positioned their buttocks into well used chairs, Fishwick producing a folder of documents.

"No idea what you're doing here. In fact I don't know why I'm here," I retorted sternly, as I quickly scribbled my reply onto the foolscap.

Pickles appeared perplexed at my antics and was wise enough to figure out the reason why.

"There's no need for this carry-on. We're straight cops; we're not like the cowboys from Merseyside or that lot of crooks from the Met," he proclaimed with the sincerity of a used car salesman. This form of self-appraisal didn't wash with me, accepting the uncorroborated word of a crime squad inspector was tantamount to an invitation to dine with a tribe of starving cannibals, you'd be eaten alive.

"I don't want to listen to your bullshit. Do what you came to do or fuck off," I responded diplomatically, pausing to write down verbatim my reply. Consumed with fury Pickles turned to chicken faced Fishwick...

"Read out the charge sheet to him!" he commanded angrily to his partner. Fishwick nervously fiddled with some documents before focusing on his monologue. He rambled on, stating that between certain dates, stemming from a time I was incarcerated and had been so for many years, I had conspired with others to rob from six sorting officers. Stealing a sum in excess of a million pounds. A charge sheet was then handed to me by the eager Fishwick. I gave the document a cursory glimpse to confirm in my mind the dates of the alleged conspiracy, realising that the sleuths had miscalculated my whereabouts and this manufactured indictment was doomed to failure. Perhaps the self-proclaimed honest cop believed that I sprouted wings and flew over the prison wall. "Do you have anything to say?" Pickles enquired as his brown-nosed puppet completed his duty.

"Load of bollocks, Sherlock!" I said, continuing to write down my responses. He shook his head confidently, seeing me as a convenient rung in the police promotional ladder.

"Would you be prepared to answer a list of forty questions Tom? It might help your case in the long run," chirped in Fishwick in a sing-song friendly voice, a questionnaire held in his bony fingers like a hymn sheet.

"Are they them?" I asked, mimicking his phony drawl and pointing to the questionnaire in his hand.

"Yes. It won't take long," he cooed, thinking that he was luring me into an incriminating conversation. I reached over and snatched the papers out of his hand and began to tear them up. Fishwick stood there dumbstruck, Pickles ran around attempting to retrieve them. I jumped up throwing the questionnaire out of the window. Sherlock Pickles was raging like a tornado, the Screw took my part picking up my foolscap paper and pen and thus calling a halt to the interview. Pickles scolded Fishwick for being so lackadaisical and then adjusted his sights on me.

"You're going down for these crimes, you piece of Scouse shit," he threatened, his tone laced with bitterness.

"Piss off back to your cattle rustlers and your sheep-shagging boozin' mates, Sherlock-fuckin'-Holmes," I roared at the sleuth as the Screw guided me out of the room and out of earshot of the two frustrated cops. When I reached the unit I got the Screw to sign the foolscap paper as a record of my responses to the detectives probing in the event they had verballed me up. I later discovered that my co-accused of the robbery at Worcester were also indicted on an all-embracing conspiracy charges by Holmes and his intrepid colleague Dr. Fishwick. A group meeting was essential to prepare a defence against these further, if somewhat flawed conspiracy charges. A meeting that was thwarted every step of the way by ingrained bureaucratic paranoia.

Friday morning arrives and it's time for the weekly jamboree that preceded a court appearance at Worcester Magistrates'. A horse box subdivided into numerous small secure compartments would pull alongside the unit's exit, we were ushered in forthwith and driven promptly out of the prison gates to be met by the West Midlands Seventh Cavalry, an armed posse of siren-blaring cop cars, motor-cyclist outriders and even a helicopter above. All that was missing was a brass marching band. This convoy of adrenalin pumped up storm troopers charged flat out to our courtroom destination pausing for nothing and no one. Snipers stood on the rooftops of buildings close to the courthouse; armed cops flitted about the hallways searching everyone with unbridled enthusiasm - even solicitors and official cleaners were patted down. We were eventually located together in a cell in the dungeons of this judicial tomb; this was the first time I had actually conversed and met the group since the fiasco of a robbery. Serious questions needed to be answered as to the depths of our predicament and how an entire police force was forewarned that a crime was to take place. Identifying the Judas in our midst was not as clear cut as it first seemed because the main protagonist was under the protective umbrella of a Chief Constable. An unknown factor at the time. The five of us scanned the cell thoroughly searching for listening devices but we detected nothing visible to the naked eye. We debated our precarious situation and the additional indictment levelled against us.

"As far as I'm concerned we've been set up here. Some dirty bastard pawned us," I announced to my accomplices who more or less shared this observation. A tidal wave of curses and violent threats abounded turning the air blue as one and all vented their anger at our misfortune.

"Who the fuck knew besides us that we going on this bit of graft?" asked Billy putting the question to the gathering of angry captives.

"Fat fuckin' Sid, for one," I nominated in response to his query. A silence descended as they contemplated the possibility of Fatso being guilty of digging our graves. Jay and Jon appeared to nod in agreement but Vinnie, and Billy to a lesser degree refused to accept this hypothesis.

"You're way off the fuckin' mark mate," Vinnie asserted, defending his business partner.

"No way Tom. He's sound," chipped in Billy, supportive of his brother and the Machiavellian Fat Sid.

"Who else can it be then?" pondered the reticent Jay who like me suspected Fat Sid of doing the dirty deed from day one.

A heated debate ensued as we attempted to discover the cause of a breach in the pre-robbery security. I reemphasised my stance adding that nobody outside this cell was aware of my involvement other than Fat Sid. Further scrutiny of the bona fides of associates of the gang took place during the forthcoming months as we hoped to prove who took the thirty pieces of silver. In the meantime our efforts were concentrated on the legal aspects of the indictments. Keys jangling in the door served to interrupt the discussion and a Screw popped his head into the cell.

"Right chaps, they're ready for yer," he bawled, stepping aside to allow us to be manhandled, cuffed and taken into the dock. Entering the courtroom was, I imagined, the equivalent to appearing live on stage at some Gilbert and Sullivan opera; the scene was awash with colour, Mad Mannering was bobbing up and down orchestrating gun-toting plod into position; the gallery was bursting at the seams, brimming with students from a nearby university; the well of the dock was a hornets nest of solicitors, clerks and police barristers anxiously shuffling papers. I expected a round of applause with all the participants bursting into song. The clerk of the court was dwarfish in stature, a thick bush of silver hair crowned his cabbage shaped head; aged about sixty he bossed the performance. A trio of magistrates perched on a throne behind him, like three blackbirds looking for food. We stood in the dock as the clerk addressed us individually before reciting the indictment. The trio of magistrates reacted accordingly by huddling together whispering words of wisdom in each other's ears then turning to us, whereupon they would remand us in custody for another seven days. A procedure that dragged on for nine months until we were eventually arraigned for trial. The delay was created by the ineptitude of Sherlock Pickles and Dr. Fishwick as they sought to prove a convoluted conspiracy theory. After suffering this mindless nonsense for months we decided to liven up the weekly pantomime and relieve the monotony with futile bail applications. Each week one of us would apply for bail either via a solicitor or through a personal appeal to the Bench. A police barrister would then spring up opposing the frivolous bail request - a ritual that attracted a local admiration society that jammed into this judicial theatre's public gallery for each performance. The cabbage headed clerk, halted the application process on one occasion to order the removal of female supporters from the gallery for exposing their breasts. Mannering's Muppets stampeded into the audience and frog marched the screeching girls off the premises to a rousing chorus of jeers.

One week as the rites were concluded, the question was put to the prosecution barrister if he could indicate how long before committal proceedings and a subsequent trial date. He contemplated this simple request for a little while, spun around to face the dock, to utter a curt sarcastic reply. "How long is a piece of string?" A torrent of abuse rained down on his bewigged dome, castigating his sexuality and his legal pedigree. He truly regretted that riposte; we christened him Mr. Metaphor and from that day forth he became the brunt of numerous courtroom jokes. Bail applications had become absurd and increasingly outrageous, much to the annoyance of the principle antagonists. Billy quoted laws from the Magna Carta, the execution of innocent men, the inhumane prison conditions, the deafness of the Bench, in the first of his nipping bail bids.

"Was there any truth in the rumour," I asked Mr. Metaphor, "that the excessive and barbaric security measures imposed upon us, stem from intelligence reports that we started the Vietnam War after killing J.F. Kennedy?" This Question was the crux of a bail request. He gave a terse response - "Absolute poppycock!" The game was getting to him.

These day trips provided a therapeutic distraction from the rigor of life in the jailhouse sewers. Locking antlers each week with the Worcester legal system boosted our morale, more so when they took the ludicrous banter seriously, adhering to an inbred political correctness. We usually fell about laughing. Our goose was already cooked, so fuck 'em.

CHAPTER 5

Beatings of mainstream prisoners by The Jowl and his horde of muscle-bound mules happened on a regular basis. The brutalisation of these unfortunate souls began by dragging them down an iron staircase onto the quadrant outside our cells; the extent of their beating coincided with the gravity of their misconduct. An assault on a Screw resulted in a good thrashing until the recipient was comatose. The Murder of Barry Prosser was a classic example of the vicious punishment dished out by the thugs.

I was lying on my bunk reading a book during the late afternoon when the shrieks of someone pleading for mercy pierced the air sending shivers down my spinal column. I leapt to my feet and headed for the cell door, pushing the Judas spy hole back with a pencil. A sickening sight played out in the quadrant; a screaming inmate was being booted and severely beaten by a band of warders; he was crying out in vain to God for help as kicks and punches rained down on his battered and bloodied body. I began smashing at the door, bawling at the merciless bastards to leave him alone; the other prisoners in this isolation unit were in uproar, forced to endure the sounds of the beating. We all suffered behind locked doors listening to the shrieks of agony from inmate Prosser. Prosser was bounced along the passageway, stripped of all clothes and hurled unconscious into a cell. Voices littered the airwaves as prisoners bayed through cell windows detailing the savage beating inflicted against the defenceless inmate. I stood with my ear to the doorjamb. A flock of Screws were milling about boasting to each other about their heroic actions.

"That prick wasn't so fuckin' hard. Like a baby after I smashed em on the head," a Screw's voice rasped, generating a symphony of laughter.

"These fuckin' scumbags gotta understand, fuck with us an' we'll kick the shit out of yer," echoed another staunch supporter of law and order. The audience mumbled in harmony to his bold statement. The conversation continued in this vein for a few minutes, the culprits vomiting forth with their gory accounts of this appalling act.

"What the fuck av you done? Get that fuckin' blood wiped up," yelled a voice, disrupting the thugs' ego party. It was S.O. Muat who was in charge of the unit on this particular day. It was The Jowls day off.

"The bastard had it comin' boss. He shoved one of us," responded one of the pack, justifying their savagery. "Shut up dickhead, just get the fuckin' mess cleaned," ranted Muat, aware of the atmosphere of hostility ricocheting throughout the unit. I took a sly peek out of the Judas hole and spied on the shower of rabid dogs mopping the bloodstains off the floor and walls. As I watched, it began to dawn on me that this latest act of violence had been far more lethal than most. The vicious bastards were covering their guilt-ridden backs. A mainstream convict usually dealt with all cleansing requirements. It wasn't long before my suspicions were confirmed. Mealtime proved particularly harrowing in the aftermath of the beating; a heavy presence of intimidatory Screws formed a gauntlet leading from the cell to the food hot-plate. A stifling atmosphere prevailed, not a word was spoken. All in the unit were fed and banged up in record time. A few hours later Prosser's door was unlocked by a brace of Screws. Their dialogue was overheard by Jay.

"Get off the floor, get off the fuckin' floor!" a voice rising in tempo and urgency. There was no response from the lifeless Prosser. A daunting silence gripped the unit as we strained, earholes glued to the door jambs. He's fuckin' dead. The bastard's gone an' died on us," a Screw wailed, assigning blame to the deceased. Slamming the door shut, they both hastily departed the scene. They soon returned with in-house medical staff who swiftly disposed of the body. The news of Prosser's brutal demise came as no surprise to me, witnessing first-hand the propensity for violence offered by these Gestapo pit bulls. It was a miracle the mortality rate wasn't a good deal higher, such was the subculture of fear and brutality incubated and encouraged during this period of unruliness. A feeble minded arsonist who's task it was to clean the unit's toilets and mop floors appeared to have witnessed the assault and contacted us by slipping notes under our doors naming the killers. This data was stored and eventually smuggled to Prosser's family. Nonetheless, exposing the culpability of those involved was prioritised by our group. A jailhouse priest popped into my cell a few days after the murder. He was a grubby looking creature who sported a tatty unkempt beard; the face fuzz was littered with small particles of food and tobacco. I am a secular person by nature with little time for Biblical fairy tales and the theologians who peddle the guff. The first thing that pierced my mind was a family tragedy, I associated jailhouse priests with the Grim Reaper but it was purely a social visit to see if I required any religious help from the Church. I suggested it would beneficial to my well-being if he could conjure up a miracle or two. He guffawed like an ass at my retort. I tested his morality before he departed to his holy fantasy land.

"Are you aware that a man was battered to death outside this door the other day," I asked him, whispering softly to avoid alerting the loitering Screws. He was sitting on the edge of the metal bed, I was standing with my back against the wall. His face iced over and his body became rigid; this topic was taboo.

"I'm sorry Smith I cannot discuss that incident. I'm here

on Church matters," he dribbled his reply, anxious to decamp picking his black Bible off the bed.

"It wasn't an incident, it was a brutal murder carried out by these three prison officers," I proclaimed, handing him a small piece of paper naming the perpetrators of the deed. He panicked, praying for the Good Lord to evoke a miracle and whisk him away to the sanctuary of his pulpit and his religious merry-go-round.

"Please Smith, I can't meddle in internal disciplinary issues. It's not permitted," he cried, pushing the piece of paper away as if I'd handed him a grenade with the pin pulled out.

"Why don't you and the so called Christian Church you represent expose the villainy that goes on in here instead of burying your holy fuckin' heads in sand?" I inquired to the apostles hasty retreating back. He was about to slam the door when he paused and swivelled his head in a semicircle, checking as to the whereabouts of the thugs then poked his holy head back through the slightly ajar door, and spoke.

"I would reveal the iniquities that go on in this prison to the appropriate authorities tomorrow but I'm afraid any interference from the church would result in us being banned. I can do more good being of spiritual assistance to the needy prisoners," he vowed as if he were preaching to a congregation of mindless morons. He banged the door before I had chance to respond to his guff. He vanished forever, gone to places where his gospel of hypocrisy would be swallowed - a true Christian. The Friday following Prosser's death, time for the weekly cabaret at the magistrates' court. The usual police lunacy as the convoy of armed police officers steamed down the motorways like formula one drivers. In the cells below the court we decided to forego the bail comedy routine and draw attention to the slaying of Prosser. When the initial ritual was done, Billy leapt to his feet...

"I am reporting a murder that was witnessed by the five of us. A murder that took place in Winston Green Prison," he announced loudly and with the utmost clarity. Instantly we all joined him, rounding on individual officers, naming the victim, the culprits, and asked what action, if any, would be taken. Two Screws, who sat in the dock with us, attempted to suppress the outburst by shoving Billy down the stairs. They lost the scuffle and ended up in the well of the court. A right melee ensued resembling a ruck on a rugby pitch rather than the sanitised tranquillity of a courtroom. Mad Mannering was bellowing out with coded references, we later thought he was trying to call on air-strikes. We refused to exit the dock until we got an official response to our allegation. Mr. Metaphor sprang to his feet like some posturing troubadour and appealed for calm.

"Return to the cells chaps and I give you my solemn word that statements will be taken from you before you leave this court today." he declared as he placed his right hand on his heart for dramatic effect. We descended to the cells at loggerheads with the Screws, who were threatening us with disciplinary action on our return to the jug. They were told to piss off and get on reading their porn magazines. Two detectives turned up and took detailed accounts of the slaying from each of us.

Jay's deposition was taken first. He described in minute detail every blow, punch and stamp on the head, kick in the kidneys, naming the aggressors responsible for each lethal strike. We all more or less corroborated this account of the killing. We duly signed the statements and were informed that they would be delivered post-haste to their colleagues at West Midlands Police, in whose jurisdiction the crime was committed. We added that we were prepared to testify under oath to the accounts in our statements. That was the last time anybody was contacted about the Prosser murder. I heard that the detectives made confetti out of the statements tossing them out of the car windows as soon as they left the court. Three officers were indicted for the death of this inmate, a vow of silence by guards, a flimsy police investigation, a bumbling half-hearted prosecution failed to secure a just verdict. They beat the original rap, convicted on some nonsensical charge of neglect and dereliction of duty. I believe they got suspended from duty for six months then transferred to a less stressful prison. A rumour bounced about the jailhouse circles that prison dog handlers named the most ferocious of dogs after the gruesome trio. Assistant Governor Knox dealt with maximum-security inmates; he took no pride in his personal appearance; it always seemed that he'd slept in his crumpled, gravy stained clothes. We nicknamed him the paraffin lamp or The Paraffin for short. He looked a lot older than his mid-twenties and dressed accordingly, a career civil servant, loved the job and the concomitant influences his position gave him. He remembered every rule and regulation and would rattle them off whenever we had a confrontation with him.

The day after the melee in the magistrates' court, we were brought before him on a catalogue of disciplinary charges. He sat behind a desk in the small office inside the unit, a flock of Screws in attendance. Vinnie was produced first and declined to participate in the silly kangaroo court and verbally abused Knox accusing him of complicity in the Prosser slaying. This stance was replicated by all involved.

"You're charged with section 063 of the penal code, that you wilfully disobeyed officers at the magistrates' court, and therein assaulted Officer Simpson. How do you plead?" Knox chanted away as I stood before him, circled by a flock of snarling uniforms, in this simulated court martial. Knox glared awaiting a response.

"You scruffy daft bastard. How do you fuckin' plead to a

blatant cover-up? Dickhead," I yelled at the immoral role-playing midget.

"Away, lock him up," he replied, unperturbed, as he gestured for the uniforms to bang me up. I was frog marched to my cell. A. G. Knox imposed the customary embargo, no bed, to make life more miserable declaring that he was powerless to inflict more punishment due to our un-convicted status. I tried to raise the issue of the recent murder being the cause of the unruly courtroom antics but he dismissed this notion out of hand. Knox and the entire administration wore blinkers and ear-plugs insofar as the brutalisation of inmates was concerned. Ray Charles, the blind jazz singer would see more than this lot. I expressed this opinion to my co-defendants, it was pointless expecting any of these bureaucrats to go against the grain. Obeying orders justifies genocide and the most heinous of atrocities; this institutionalised ideology will never be changed from within; their job is their life, the very essence of their mundane existence. Controversy that might bring the prison service into disrepute was to be avoided at all costs from the number one governor to the lowly turnkey that makes the tea. Exposing these custodians to the Left Wing media was the one and only avenue to pursue - a campaign we embarked on. Alan Hale was my solicitor; he had an eagle eye and a sharp brain for detail. Over the years we had shared a number of legal crusades, none as hopeless as this. He had made an appointment to visit me on the day of Knox's judicial simulation. He duly arrived at the scheduled time but was refused entry by the Screws, they alleged he was drunk. He had travelled from Liverpool to Birmingham by train, he had eaten a meal and consumed one glass of red wine. A Screw with the nasal senses of a blood hound; a wizard at detecting intoxication, smelt the faint aroma of alcohol and ejected Alan from the premises. Apparently the Screw became known as the human breathalysers. This nonsense was a ploy by the puerile bullying element amongst the staff to make things as awkward as possible following our courtroom outburst. A closing of ranks. I received mail from my solicitor explaining the petty shenanigans of the Winston Green mafia. He had taken legal steps to ensure that this illegal tactic wouldn't happen again, citing the governor in a writ for the obstruction of justice. A defence needed to be compiled and erected to challenge the additional conspiracy charges, otherwise the Crown will bury us alive. I needed to consult and resolve this dilemma with my legal representative, also to clarify the depth of evidence, if any, against my co-accused. A perpetual state of incommunicado would hinder our defence.

CHAPTER 6

Prison visits were monitored, a uniform sat within earshot listening for escape plots or anything slightly conspiratorial. Several months had slipped by since our capture and a river of rumours flowed our way through the jailhouse visiting rooms naming the villain who betrayed us. The most popular nominee being Fatso. A relation of the brothers, the 'Laughing Policeman', liaised with Fatso creating an active information conduit between the prison and the now extremely paranoid fat man. Fatso more than likely realised that the icy fingers of suspicion would eventually point in his direction and so he controlled the visiting arrangements, using the Laughing Policeman to exchange snippets of intelligence and to gauge the extent that the cloak of suspicion would be draped upon his flabby shoulders. The man possessed the cunning of a field full of foxes which he put to use to divert the looming spectra of hostility away from him and onto the head of an innocent man.

Once a year at the Adelphi Hotel, a charity ball takes place organised by a lodge of the Freemasons. Most of the members are police officers but it's also attended by local dignitaries and friends of the cops. The gala room of the Adelphi was a resplendent sight; a huge cavernous arena with intricate art-deco ceilings from which dangled opulent crystal chandeliers and murals adorned the walls which in those days radiated luxury.

A female relation of the clairvoyant had an invitation to the ball, arriving in the company of a prominent detective - gossip had it that this particular detective was partial to a pound note.

Fatso locked into this scenario; he knew that the relation of the clairvoyant was involved with the cop and therefore was an indirect link to me. The relation's name was Joan. The night was filled with coincidences that somehow filtered across the landscape, through the steel bars and into the cell-block of Winston Green. Ale flowed and the cops gulped it down, hoping to dislodge their helmets for a while allowing a brief period of association with a nervous and apprehensive public. Joan's escort, Detective Washbourne, appeared to be the worse for wear when two colleagues from the crime squad jostled their way onto the table ostensibly to monitor their boisterous mate. One of the pair ordered a bottle of the cheapest plonk while the other engaged Joan in idle tittle-tattle. Introducing himself as Ralph, he used his interrogation skills to put her at ease. This cop manipulated the conversation to a point where the topic of debate was karma. A grotesque masquerade unfolded. Ralph's plonk-drinking mate began reciting a tale about a paedophile who sexually abused five of his children over several years subjecting them to the vilest acts. He explained that it was the most sickening case he had ever worked on and what magnified the wickedness of this particular case was the fact, the unbelievable fact, that his wife brought the children up to visit him in jail - the very children that he had used and abused. We kicked up a fuss when we found out, notifying those useless bastards in the social services. Anyway, he continued, the beast was serving his sentence in Wakefield Prison when another prisoner by the name of Mawdsley garrotted the depraved bastard in his cell, almost decapitating him. To me that is karma, the animal danced with the devil and got his just deserts. Joan agreed, adding that the paedophile's wife was as bad as him.

"Visiting him, I wouldn't be a minute, I would set fire to the scumbag as he slept," she concluded, joining the interaction.

Ralph then interceded with a version about the precariousness of fate.

"Recently we had dealings with an informant who had given us top-level intelligence about a notorious gang of armed robbers. He had grown up in the same street as most of them and was a peripheral player in the gang's activities. He had been nicked on a minor felony charge cashing traveller's checks that were taken during a raid on a postal sorting office. We knew he wasn't capable of the robbery nevertheless we applied pressure on him and to our surprise and delight he decided to play ball. He named the members of the gang, even pinpointing the gang's next target - a postal sorting office at Worcester." Joan's antenna went on red alert, she knew of my involvement in this crime, consequently she deposited every word of the narrative into her astute memory bank and repeated it to me on a prison visit. Ralph's tale continued. "The gang's movements were shadowed and they were subsequently captured red-handed, one of the culprits was shot by our boys." Now here's where karma lurks its vengeful head; the informant was due to receive a substantial reward for his treachery which he eventually came to collect. I thanked him for his cooperation and passed him a cheque, which he refused, explaining that he didn't want a paper trail leading back to him.

This was a Friday afternoon. It was too late to get the cash and arrangements were made with him to call on Monday when the cash would be ready. In the early hours of Sunday morning the informant and his wife were pissed and crashed into a skip - both died instantly."

"My God, what a story, they say what goes around comes around," Joan said, in response to this police parable, not cracking on she was a friend of mine. The conversation carried on for a while with Joan throwing in an urban fable or two creating a cordial ambience amongst the merrymakers.

Detective Washbourne who had swilled enough booze to float a barge ordered a round of drinks and when the waitress asked for the bill he struggled to find his wallet and turned to Ralph accusing him of stealing it. Joan stepped in admonishing Washbourne, stating that Ralph was a policeman and wouldn't steal his wallet. The detective flew into a rage denouncing Ralph as a crook who was forever stealing police property - he even syphons the petrol out of the patrol cars. The drunken detective put the dampers on the evening, the party was over, the guests left for home. The pair of intrusive cops had meticulously planted the fabricated seeds of disinformation into fertile ground where the seeds then blossomed and spread thus eliminating the Fat Man as the probable traitor from the forefront of our minds. A dead man was the fertilizer used by the police to secure the safety and future alliance with this deep-rooted grass. A great many years passed by before the truth seeped through about the treachery and skulduggery that coexisted between vipers like Fatso and morally bankrupt, ambitious detectives. Fatso's confidant ended up a Chief Constable. News hit a couple of the lads hard that a close friend who had slept in their beds, eaten at each other's tables and roamed the streets together as kids would be party to such a diabolical betrayal. A week or so earlier they mourned his death. A death of convenience - something we regretfully never knew at the time. Analysing the information and its source proved difficult, although we were caged in the same jail and housed on the same wing. We only met in court on Fridays and we conversed through cell windows - conversations that were being logged. An immediate obstacle to overcome was the fact that the austere restraints imposed by the regime were preventing us from examining the conspiracy as a group. We decided to tackle the issue forthwith and a request was made to The Paraffin to accommodate us with a facility.

"I have carefully looked at your request for a facility to allow you to assemble as a group in order to prepare a defence to additional charges. I'm sorry but under rules governing A-listed prisoners, your request is denied," Knox expressed his predictable response, his grim features distorted with a self-satisfied smile. He posed in the open doorway of my cell. Two uniformed warriors stood either side of this philanthropist as he lingered in anticipation of a reaction, a reaction that would caress his frustrated mind and induce a mental orgasm. All the symptoms of masochism oozed from every pore of his deviant personality.

"Is that your good deed for the day? You fuckin' tramp," I volleyed at the flushed cheeked Knox who chuckled, then gave the door an almighty bang. He repeated the process to my fellow conspirators. A day of multiple orgasms. Billy soaked him with a cup of cold tea - an anti-climax for Knox. Having exhausted all polite approaches to access our fundamental right to confer with co-defendants in a complex conspiracy, a unanimous decision was made to go on hunger strike. We had shuffled along the penal bullshit routes, petitioning old Etonian civil servants in the Home Office who probably turned our mail into paper darts, chucking them at each other after the customary rubber stamped denial. I don't know of one prisoner who ever got a positive response to a Home Office petition. I went a step further during this harrowing period by drafting a critique to the Queen. I explained the inhumane conditions surrounding our incarceration in one of her establishments, highlighting the facts relating to the murderers and the vicious thugs that we were forced to mix with - the prison officers. This drew a blank from the good lady. In all likelihood the mail never left the jail. The crux of our grievances was simplicity itself - we were un-convicted remand-status prisoners yet we were held in solitary confinement, allowed out of our cell for one hour's exercise each day. It was essential that we had unmonitored access to each other for the purpose of mounting a defence. We were equated more or less on a par with struggling I.R.A. insurgents who were vacuum packed then buried in various cages dotted about the British gulags.

CHAPTER 7

Boney M, the sensory deprivation tool, shattered the early-morning tranquillity as The Jowl and his swashbuckling boot boys prepared for breakfast. Doors unlocked to the customary cycle of aggressive vibes generating from our tormentors, no attempt at communication, just a fusillade of glares as the meagre fayre was dumped upon stainless-steel trays, whereupon we retreated to our individual cells. Thirty minutes later the cell doors were unlocked to collect the empty trays; all our trays were untouched, the food uneaten.

"What's this bollocks then Smith?" bellowed The Jowl, strutting outside my door along with two of his boot boys. I stared at the thug as he displayed his prowess for intimidation in front of the two mentally constipated dummies.

"That bollocks, Einstein, is a tray full of shit. As from today I'm refusing food. Ok?" I responded to his belligerent request. He grimaced, anger bubbling up inside his blubbery chest. He ordered a dummy to take the tray to the office.

"I'm fuckin' sick to death of you Scouse bastards. God help you once you're convicted," he roared threateningly at me, his two paws balled into fists as he frantically beat the air.

"Piss off, you big fat fuck pig!" I replied locking onto his stony faced stare. He gave the door a hefty bang almost taking it off the hinges. His rage stemmed from strict Home Office regulations governing hunger strikers. It would involve a great deal of paperwork for The Jowl, more so when there were five protesters refusing food. He couldn't give a damn if we became human funeral pyres, he'd gladly fan the flames, all that mattered to this sub-specimen was that any extra paperwork might keep him away from his pornography.

Five trays of un-tasted slops were deposited on the desk in the wing office for eyeball verification from A.G. Knox and this bureaucratic farce was played out each mealtime. The peas would be counted, the stodgy spuds weighed, the meat scrutinised to see if it had been chewed. A cuckoo-land policy went into full swing ensuring that there was no cheating by any of the hunger strikers who may have succumbed to temptation and swallowed a couple of peas. Although we refused to eat, each mealtime a tray of food was put in our cell, left for an hour, then duly collected by forensically trained Screws who transported the tray of uneaten fayre to the wing office where it was probed and analysed. If so much as a crumb had been eaten, the nuts would scream and bawl out, "He's eaten food, the bastard's eaten something." signalling to the penal colony bosses that the fast was broken, encouraging them to manufacture a report that the strike was over.

Pangs of hunger totally dominated the conscious thought process as the first day without food drew to a close; visions of past feasts bullied the way into the mind's eye causing me to salivate like one of Pavlov's dogs. We had decided to drink water when the pangs became ravenous; I would gulp down a pint of water, then pace up and down for a while; this seemed to stifle the urge. A situational comparison with the heroin bag heads sprang to mind, a preoccupation to nourish a craving, a rampaging craving running through my brain like a steam train. Self-discipline would be one factor in combating the nagging compulsion for food. I jumped up to the window and checked on the famished four's battle against hunger. Billy and Jay answered my call.

"It's hard graft, this no food fuckin' business. How are you finding it?" I questioned the starving duo. A chorus of 'fuckin' hard mate', came echoing back.

"Stick at it! I read somewhere that you don't feel hungry after the first few days," volunteered Billy, his advice stamped with steely determination.

"I hope so Bill, I'm chewing fuckin' wood here, I'd even eat the crappy cold porridge," Jay chirped, obviously feeling the impact of the food withdrawal symptoms.

"We've started this fuckin' thing, carry on for a bit longer and see if the dogs capitulate," I suggested positively, whilst straining to maintain the momentum.

"Tom, I believe we're on the radio tomorrow, some fuckin' publicity might liven these assholes up," announced Billy injecting a modicum of optimism into the gossip. I didn't know if the snippet about the publicity was true or a propaganda ruse for the eavesdropping Screws who constantly monitored window to window dialogues.

"A nuclear missile wouldn't effect these emotional zombies mate. They've had it their own way for fuckin' years, they're immune to normal feelings," I cynically stated after years of confrontation with institutional Man. It was impossible to argue with them, they had all the answers, they were never wrong. A human-rights angle that causes embarrassment to the minister in charge may induce a shift in the intransigence of Knox forcing his grubby hands to amend his Gestapo tactics. Publicity was anathema to these penal bigots, debunking their claim to be upholders of human rights, common decency and fair play. This was the initial ploy behind a combined decision to go on a hunger strike. Time will reveal if our decision was correct or another painful error of judgment. Four days into this voluntary starvation diet, the brain's receptors had nullified the pangs of hunger and the desire for food had greatly diminished.

Radio Merseyside had broadcast our protest in its hourly news bulletin detailing our grievances; a local M.P. had raised the issue with the Home Office; graffiti denouncing the Screws was splashed on the walls of Liverpool's urban council estates; sympathizers were offering to march against the Screws and give them a dose of their own medicine. Gangsters threatened to put hits on the bullying bastards. The freedom pipelines were alive with gossip and the drumbeats of rumour about torture, beatings and poisoning. We refused to eat because they spit on the food and pissed in our tea. A tornado of response blew over the walls, uplifting any wilting spirits and hopefully helping to achieve the objective. Nothing changed the obdurate attitude within the unit, no connection to policy implementers; Knox chanted to his enforcers that if the idiots want to starve themselves to death so be it. He bellowed this at night so we could all hear his words of compassion and understanding. A voiced bayed out calling Knox a fuckin' transvestite. Fifth day was memorable for a noticeable change in the swill that was usually dished up. A proper full English breakfast was delivered to each of our cells, something I'd never seen in a prison before; the food was piping hot, a unique phenomenon and as regular as an eclipse of the Moon. This tactic should have been deployed the second or third day - we might have succumbed to temptation and taken the bait. Time had eroded the initial fixation to eat during the first few days, although physically weaker we seemed to be mentally stronger. A grim determination had hustled into our psyche. The sumptuous, mouth-watering breakfast was rejected by one and all, much to the surprise of The Jowl. He could be heard cursing the cooks for wasting good food on Scouse bastards. Nevertheless the meals throughout the day would appease the palate of the most discerning of gourmets. Lunch was steak, chips, mushrooms, peas with a black forest gateau for desert. A kidnapping of a restaurateur by the Screws was our explanation for these dishes as cooking food was deemed to be beyond the scope of jailhouse chefs. Again, the food was refused sending The Jowl's temperature soaring through the unit's roof. Sixth day, we here now exempt from the one-hour daily exercise. The cell became a tomb and to add impetus to the dispute we decided to go on The Blanket. This demonstration of solidarity entailed pursuing a regime of non-compliance by discarding clothes and bedding, using the cell as a toilet, urinating and crapping on the floors, refusing to wash or shave - a descent into the very pits of degradation, a personal debasement that tested the core of my self-respect. The Blanket was a tool utilised by Republican prisoners in The Maze prison to enhance their claims for political prisoner status. Accomplishing political recognition wasn't on our agenda, just a portion of common sense and parity with other remand prisoners instead of the austere measures foisted upon us by Winston Green's Spartan regime. Streams of urine trickled beneath the doors onto the highly polished floors of the quadrant disrupting the rigid order and discipline embedded in the brains of The Jowl and his troops. This was his fiefdom, he was judge, jury and executioner, unchallenged and seemingly above reproach in this penal bubble but the stench of human waste was inciting discontent amongst this stalwart pack of masters of misery. Arguments escalated as officers declined to mop up the mess; one or two of them walked out feigning sickness. Threats of extreme violence filled the air. "You will pay for this you dirty Scouse bastards," was repeated throughout the day. The dawn of the second day of the dirty protest and the cell resembled a pig pen; we were living like wild animals, there was no escaping the filth - it attacked the nostrils nauseating the senses, the lungs gasping for a dose of cool clear oxygen. Doors were unlocked at world record speed, a tray of food and a jug of water placed on the urine stained floor, the door slammed within the blink of an eye. There was a noticeable absence of taunting and venomous glares. All the Screws wore surgeon's masks in a crude effort to staunch inhaling the malodorous fumes fouling their workplace. Tempers were fraying, the androids complaining loud and clear about the conditions. Unrest reigned but no compromise, no dialogue, nothing to persuade or dissuade us from continuing on the path to insanity; later, after suppertime, a voice was yelling from the main prison.

"Hey Scouse you're on the telly. It's on the news about yer. Don't let the bastards get yer down." A stranger with a Brummie accent informed us that we had made it to the news channels. I clambered to the window gasping the sweet air into my lungs before calling out to my weary mates. "Vinnie, did you hear that?" I proclaimed relating to the unknown voice.

"I got it, wonder what garbage the pricks said about us," he replied, conveying a mood of disenchantment that was creeping into our camp.

"I don't know, it can only help our cause. These bastards hate any kind of exposure, they can't stand any publicity, there's too many skeletons hidden about in these karsey's mate," I responded, injecting a touch of hope into the dark chilling caves we were now wandering in.

"The shit is getting to 'em, the slags are screamin' like fuck at each other. A few more days an' this bollocks is done," he replied, sounding as if, like the rest of us, he was becoming exhausted with this ordeal. I descended from the window, shrank into a corner of my toilet bowl of a cell, and fell into a semi-comatose trance, spirits plummeting into an abyss of despair. I scribbled on a wall…

Shrinking strangling stifling gasping for air,
Castrated cursed chastened but does anyone care?
Alone all alone I suffer this pitiless plight,
The only relief, the black blanket of the night.
The seeds you sow bestow the sorrow you know.
Paths I tread blood I shed, lead to this mortal moment of dread.
What lies ahead for this worthless soul, misery madness a fiery hole?
I weep in my sleep for the threads I let be
and for that life I'll never see.
As the weary end draws nigh and I expel the ultimate sigh,
Will one soul laugh or cry or even utter a mournful goodbye?
A meaningless sham the path I trod wanton wasteful devoid of God.
The shadows there since birth vanish as they must
and I return to a handful of dust.

The gloomy despair was only as transient as the mayfly, lasting a night. Apparently the national television news channels had broadcast that five men had started a 'dirty protest' at Winston Green; in the report they made a situational comparison with the 'H-Blocks' in Northern Ireland. This sparked a new approach by the administration towards us - an exchange of civil dialogue with a marked absence of malice. An unfamiliar face visited all of us in our cells with a proposition that if we ceased the dirty protest, a Home Office representative would meet us to discuss our grievances immediately. We insisted that we be allowed to discuss it as a group beforehand and the request was agreed on the spot. After a brief meeting, bare-arsed except for a blanket, a temporary truce was announced; we all showered off, drank a cup of tea and awaited the arrival of a 'Man' bringing common sense to the table. We eventually rendezvoused in the prison chapel as the unit stank to the high heavens; we insisted that The Jowl and any of his boot boys should be barred from the debate which was accepted much to The Jowl's irritation. A young man, elegantly dressed and with an Oxford accent listened to our complaints, then spoke softly to a prison governor, who made a note of his suggestions. We spent almost an hour with this particular Home Office trouble-shooter; he was extremely polite and treated us with respect and understanding.

"As from today you will be moved out of the segregation unit to a secure annex; each afternoon you will be allowed to congregate in a cell for a period of two hours for recreational purpose, or legal matters. A new regime of officers will be in charge of the annex. I give you my word on this." He announced this with conviction and authority. He then rose shook hands with the governor who looked as if he'd lost his wallet as well as losing face in front of us. A brace of Screws then escorted us to the annex, which turned out to be a decent move, with decent humans bossing the show. It was comparable to a move from Bradford to Barbados, the place had been treated to a lick of fresh paint, everywhere was spick and span, the cells were spotless, the bedding clean, the staff sociable and accessible, the ablutions spacious and modern - even the food had improved and was served hot. The snarling pit bulls remained in their segregation fiefdom, doubtlessly still terrifying and torturing those who fell foul of penal law. We never crossed swords with any of them again. The annex's primary function was to contain mentally ill prisoners but lack of an adequate isolation area for category 'A' inmates pushed these prisoners onto the back burner and the annex became a welcome facility for 'A' men. I settled down for the night in this much enlightened environment - a small red security light glowing in the ceiling and I drifted off into a deep sleep. Suddenly, I was awakened by something crawling on my chest, I leapt up grabbing at this uninvited creature, it squealed and fell onto the floor, it was a mouse, the pristine cell was alive with mice. I picked up a chair and gave the door an almighty whack, a Screw rushed to my aide.

"Get me out of here. It's fuckin crawling with rats," I yelled still half asleep as I spoke with the Screw who was waiting for assistance to arrive.

"Stay calm Smith, It's only mice, they're harmless," he said attempting to pacify me.

"Harmless, they're dancing all over my fuckin' chest," I bellowed, waking up all residents in the annex.

"Ok, ok, I'll open you up now." Two Screws opened me up, pulling my bed out looking for the mouse. One of them explained that the mouse had crawled through an air vent on the outer wall, and to prevent further intrusions I should block it up with newspaper. I followed his advice, consequently my sleep was never invaded again. A couple of days later the Screw was guiding the clairvoyant to the visiting room and joked about my image as a hardened criminal being scared of a mouse. She found it highly amusing; I found it disturbing. Senior Officer Morris commanded the annex; he had served for a number of years in the Royal Navy; he introduced himself to us.

"I am a fair man, I run a steady ship here, you'll get treated the same as other prisoners, what you're entitled to you will get, any complaints, see me and I will deal with them impartially. Any questions?" He addressed us as if we were the crew on a battleship and needless to say, he became known as Captain Birdseye from that day forth. Morris was indeed a fair man; there was no hostility or signs of intimidation, no insane music blaring out in the morning; it was totally the opposite to the fiefdom of The Jowl and his gang of boot boys. I believe that if we had remained under the auspices of The Jowl, one of the five of us would have met a brutal death albeit 'accidental' or suffered serious injuries.

CHAPTER 8

Tackling the Crown Prosecution's indictment occupied our time as we read through the deposition evidence. Worcester was a fait accompli, additional conspiracy charges would increase jail time considerably if proven. Evidence of my personal culpability in the conspiracy was non-existent but still caused me grave concern. I had no faith in the bewigged judicial magicians who, using Latin esoteric terms could turn night into day before your very eyes; this trick baffled most of the eleven-plus failure jurors who would promptly and unhesitatingly deliver a guilty verdict. Guilt or innocence was inconsequential, impressing the twelve dudes squatting in the free view box was all that mattered. Defeating this indictment was a battle we could not afford to lose. The novelty of mixing together after months of social deprivation felt like the mad hatter's tea party. A chance to catch up on gossip and criminal enterprises, exchange opinions, conjure up a solution to our dilemma - a taste of normality. First consensus of opinion was to formulate an escape plan, an impossibility for an A-listed prisoner. Steve McQueen, with his entire escape committee could not bust out of here. In transit to court would require a battalion of paratroopers in conjunction with heavy artillery to effect an escape. Accepting the consequences of a crime you have committed is difficult enough but when you are a non-participant in a criminal act and held to account for it, the impact on one's mental equilibrium can be devastating, a route to Broadmoor. Escape was out of the question - mitigate the Worcester crime, and fight the conspiracy was the only option available.

A committal date duly arrived, the legal process to ascertain if there is a prima facie case for a trial. We opted for a full committal proceeding wherein we could challenge the prosecution's case and also cross-examine any witnesses called upon by the Crown. We assembled in a communal cell beneath the courthouse with legal reps buzzing about like a team of pickpockets, their advice ridiculed for being factual. Billy sacked his brief and decided to defend himself. I was adamant that we shouldn't oppose the conspiracy allegation at this stage because of the glaring flaws in the Crown's case; instead we should contest the Worcester case indictment on the grounds of entrapment. A frivolous but vital ploy if we were to achieve the main objective, getting the conspiracy charge kicked out of court. At this juncture, disclosing the fact that I was incarcerated when two of the robberies were committed would be counter-productive as the Crown would ask for a postponement which would be granted by the trio of crows on the Bench, allowing the Crown to amend the indictment and omit the two robberies. After hours of argument this strategy was agreed and finally the committal proceedings commenced. A voice shouted ready, strike up the band. A packed house awaited our appearance in the dock, the trio of magistrates were dressed to kill; Mannering was like a ballroom dancer waltzing all over the place looking for a sniper; the clerk checked his script prior to conducting the drama; solicitors, barristers prosecutors were crammed into the well of the court brimming with self-importance, shuffling documents, scribbling notes and pouring water into glasses. A charade, the masquerade players jostling for position, a myriad of supporting cast flitting hither and thither, tension etched on their faces. This was their F.A. Cup final; we all strenuously denied the charges and pleaded not guilty. The Crown's case was articulated by the admirable Mr Metaphor, who described the raid as well organised by ruthless and determined criminals. Billy, who represented himself, was copiously compiling notes on a pad supplied by the court. Opening gambits concluded, a detective swore the oath and began describing his role in our capture, expanding on operational details. None of the legal teams disputed his evidence. Billy cross examined him.

"Tell me this officer, when were you made aware of the plot to rob the sorting office? Billy spoke sternly, grasping the rail of the dock and waved his notepad at him. You could see the contempt in the detectives face having to answer questions posed by a felon. The officer hesitated before replying, eyeballing the prosecutor, who nodded affirmatively.

"I was briefed on Friday night, two days before the actual robbery," he reluctantly claimed, sighing heavily and squirming with obvious frustration.

"You knew before the fact that an ambush was planned? Why didn't you or any of the squad prevent us entering the premises?" Billy enquired putting him on the spot.

Mr Metaphor interceded, rescuing the officer from what might embarrass the gung-ho tactics of the police. He addressed the clerk.

"This line of questioning has no bearing on the culpability of the accused in this offence. With respect the defendant is heading into a cul-de-sac."

He rotated his law-book head, glaring disdainfully at the dock praying we would turn to stone. Obviously the clerk agreed, advising Billy to redirect his questioning to the actual facts. I jumped up in support of Billy.

"A pre-planned bushwhacking by a team of police gun-slingers is relevant. We were shepherded and corralled from Liverpool to Worcester by a horde of cops. This in layman's language constitutes entrapment by that officer and his loose cannon mates. The cowboys could have arrested us at any time.

If anybody is guilty it's the police," I bawled loudly at the Clerk, the prosecutor and the trio of clueless crows.

"Any more outbursts Mr Smith and you will be removed from the courtroom," proclaimed the clerk sternly, delighted with his contribution to the farce. Spectators in the public gallery applauded my eruption, irritating the strait-laced officials who threatened to eject them. Giggling girls from a nearby college gave a loud raspberry at the warning causing further disruption as Mannering's men dragged them out.

"By allowing us to enter the premises you endangered the lives of postal workers. Is it not your duty to protect the public?" Billy suggested to the clearly agitated detective. Again the prosecution objected to this line of questioning. Again his objection was upheld.

Billy pursued his act getting nowhere fast. A tribe of tiresome claptrap forensic specialists trotted in using science to place us all on the roof, photographs of us captured red-handed, a cocktail of undisputable corroborating evidence churned out in boring drab soporific tones, sending everyone to sleep. Vinnie jumped up, disturbing the daydreaming atmosphere.

"We don't want to hear all this shit. Nobody here is denying being on the job, yer shower of woolly back clowns!" Vinnie screamed loudly, fed up with courtroom protocol. A startled clerk almost fell off his bench as he reacted to another show of dissent. He ordered him to be removed. With that we all exited the dock and the trial was adjourned for the day.

Days of jurisprudence twaddle neared a conclusion when the gun-toting cop who shot me was called to give evidence. He scuttled to the box, stood there every inch a craven insecure muppet; he rattled off the oath in a barely audible whisper.

"Speak up Prick," I shouted angrily from the dock feeling animosity towards this man who had tried to kill me out of sheer terror and unbridled panic. Up popped the clerk to admonish me, warning I'd be ejected from the proceedings. I settled down listening to his account of the crime and his heroic action. A repetitive format was recited by this gunslinger until he arrived at the point where he shot me. At this juncture I wrote several questions down on foolscap and handed it to my counsel.

"The accused was carrying a stick when you came across him, (A wooden stave a meter in length, exhibit number 18A was produced and summarily waved about). He claims he froze, lowering the stick as a sign of surrender yet you opened fire at point blank range almost killing my client. Can you explain that please, officer?" Q.C. Wolfe succinctly asked the shooter, causing him to nervously loosen his tie as he searched inside his head for justification. Admitting he had panicked or that his 'bottle' evaporated would not enter onto his personal radar. All eyes were directed on his colourless face in anticipation of what reasoning he would evoke using an infinite repertoire of police justifiable use of force defences. No doubt the fact that the postal worker was hovering close by me witnessing the incident prevented a gun being planted in my hand.

"I heard D.C.I Fishwick screaming out to get a gun down here, I ran towards his voice fearing the worst; there was a lot of shouting going on; I turned into an aisle where I confronted one of the robbers; the robber I now know to be Smith." He paused for a few moments for dramatic effect which to our cynical minds compounded the lie about to be spun. "I pointed my firearm at him issuing the command to get down on the floor several times; he ignored my instructions. Smith levelled the stave at me as if to discharge what I assumed was a shotgun; thinking that lives were in danger I had no option but to fire; I believe the defendant was hit in the chest and forearm." The constable recited his well-rehearsed fairy tale to a disbelieving ensemble in the courtroom with a painful looking grin on his face. I felt the rage surging through my body at this blatant distortion of the facts. Counsel turned around and intimated for me to calm down. He had heard my mutterings of vitriolic discontent.

"I presume that you have been trained specifically for the role as a firearms officer?" counsel enquired of the constable.

"Yes, I am a member of the highly trained firearm tactical support team," he stated proudly, moving his torso in a semicircle seeking admirers.

"Twenty-twenty vision is a priority, wouldn't you say?" Wolfe suggested to the eager boastful constable.

"Yes. Every officer selected has perfect vision and I might add, a top-class marksman too," he declared, relieved to be describing his career and his elite position. Wolfe held a small black and white plastic pen in his hand, waved it in the air with a flourish. He was approximately five metres away from the witness box.

"What colour would you say this pen is?" Wolfe asked the officer.

"Black and white," answered the plod smartly.

"What material would you say it was made of?" counsel enquired of the officer. "Plastic, of course," he replied, quick as a flash.

"Obviously your vision is A1. You are able to recognize minute details from a distance of five metres. Yet constable! (He roared loudly) on the night in question you mistook a piece of wood, (He picked up the stave and shook it vigorously at the cop.) this lump of wood for a gun, then you callously pumped bullets into a suspect who had practically surrendered to you! A man standing no less than two meteres away." Wolfe's voice gathering in volume and emphasis has he concluded his allegation.

The prosecutor leapt to his feet in defence of the gunslinger, objecting hysterically. Old cabbage head was flabbergasted, he had little experience with a big city attorney, he began gulping down water. The constable's face was poppy red, agitation gripped him like a vice, mumbling away to one of Mannering's body guards.

"It wasn't like that, a robbery was going down, a red alert had been called," a flustered constable shouted out to no one in particular.

"I put it to you officer that you lost control of yourself and by doing so you deliberately intended to execute my client, thereby dispensing with the rule of law." Wolfe abruptly laid into the officer for his failings under pressure. He exposed him as an imposter. The prosecution would not suffer this line of examination any longer. He claimed that the officer was not on trial. The shooting doesn't detract from the overwhelming evidence against the accused standing in that dock. The clerk agreed with him allowing the cornered officer to squirm off the hook. Vinnie and Billy angrily disagreed with this decision slagging the clerk, criticising his allegiances to the soot-juggling constable. A heated squabble exploded involving Mannering's tactical team, the warders and the five in the dock cheered on by the students in the public gallery. Tempers boiled to a manic pitch; a warder gripped Vinnie's arm who retaliated by wrestling him to the floor. Billy grappled with a courthouse usher and I took off a shoe and flung it at the gunslinger, striking him hard on the head - he crumbled in a heap screeching loudly like a piglet being castrated. Reinforcements arrived taking us from the dock to the subterranean dungeons below. The door slammed leaving five irate robbers to reflect on another catastrophic day in the dock.

"That fuckin' dwarf might as well wear a police tunic; any

Old Bill struggling with lies and the prick steps in to save 'em," Vinnie ranted adrenalin coursing through his veins after the scuffle.

"Nothin' but a shower of assholes. Yer brief had 'em cornered there Tom, a bit longer and the prick would 'av confessed," Billy declared, upset that the scene never played out to its conclusion.

"If they had the prick on film putting a bullet in the back of our heads, it would be ruled justifiable homicide, there'd be handing out fuckin' fistfuls of medals for a heroic act," I stated cynically, fully aware that our tactics were futile; we were participating in a game of legal bullshit. The mantle of recidivists virtually alienated us from the due process of law.

"So be it, let's not make it easy for the bent bastards," Vinnie snapped, still agitated and prowling the cell like a caged lion.

"Fuck it. Get this shit over with here, what fuckin' happens afterwards, happens," Billy asserted with a philosophical shrug of his shoulders, attuned to the poor choices on offer.

Several hours elapsed as we conversed in that holding cell. A Screw related to us that legal arguments and submissions were playing out in the courtroom in our absence. Our defence strategy was erected on sand; entrapment is not a feasible argument in British law, however it can be utilised in a mitigation plea, thereby influencing the severity of a custodial sentence. Clinging to capricious threads was an emotional crutch often constructed by prisoners to dissolve the harsh realities of life. Entrapment and mitigation were the threads we foolishly adhered to during this pre-trial period. Tarot cards and chicken feathers would have been more appropriate. A distant voice calling for the prisoners to be produced alerted us that we were appearing next. On we strode into the amphitheatre, the crows listened intensely as the clerk recited our names prior to the magistrates addressing us.

"You will be remanded to the crown court for trial on all charges on the indictment," the old hag pronounced firmly. The relief was obvious on the trio's faces, their patience battered by weekly conflict situations that arose each time we gazed at them perched aloft on their judicial thrones.

A thumbs down sign summed up the drama perfectly as we hastily departed to an ovation from the students. Instead of returning to Winston Green we were shipped to Risley Remand Centre a penal hovel near Warrington. Secrecy prevailed - we were kept in the dark about the relocation to Grizzly Risley, another of Mad Mannering's master strokes. Applying logic to his paranoid obsession with security matters would bemuse the head of the C.I.A. The Screws were fuming at him. They had a darts match that night and weren't told of the change of destination until the last minute, Risley adding four or five hours to their expected journey. Risley provided a break, a change of scenery and personnel, and easier access for visitors. The majority of the clientele were un-convicted, awaiting trial for their misdemeanours, a regime that wasn't geared to busting a sinner's balls. It compared with the cheap chalet holiday camps that flourished in the seventies, disinfectant combined with stale cabbage assaulted the nostrils the moment the gates were shut. The bedding was a lot cleaner at this retribution centre than some of the Pontins stomping grounds I had flopped down in.

CHAPTER 9

Due to the category 'A' tag, we were not allowed to associate with the general population, our whereabouts were constantly monitored, and a book was signed by the warders every fifteen minutes identifying specific locations. Jay and I found ourselves on a different wing to the other members of the Worcester quintet. During the night a tremendous amount of screaming and endless banging disrupted my sleep; I thought a riot or an escape was taking place. Codeye, a night watchman, who I recognised from a previous period of incarceration, sidled up to my door.

"Tee, Tee," he called softly through the Judas hole, "You awake mate?"

I approached the door still half asleep and somewhat curious.

"Who's that?" I responded wearily.

"It's me Codeye," he whispered, "Listen your mates have barricaded in and smashed holes in the walls. The three of them are penned up together creating havoc," he informed me nervously.

"Fucksake, what's all that about?" I asked puzzled by their actions. This was a cushy place compared to the Winston Green cesspit.

"They located them on the nonce wing. Your mates wouldn't wear it and wrecked the place," he recited breathlessly.

"Can you fuckin' blame them? How stupid can you get? The fuckin' idiots," I declared disgusted at the sheer idiocy of planting them amongst sexual deviants. Nonces are viewed as subhuman and detested by all criminals. To be caged within the vicinity of such beasts violates the integrity and attacks the masculinity of men who possess a modicum of common decency.

"I know Tee, I know. It's those ex-army blokes in reception, none of 'em have any idea how to deal with you guys. Look, I'll have to go. I can't do anything for you, cos of this category 'A' lark," he responded amicably, then quietly vanished into the night.

Codeye got his nickname after he was stabbed in the eye by an inmate whilst checking on him through the Judas hole. A psychopathic Congolese, riddled with mental abnormalities and awaiting a deportation order to return him to his homeland, was advised by a fellow prisoner that he could avoid deportation by an act of gross violence. Meanwhile his abnormal behaviour, such as barking like a dog and biting people or covering his head with food was ignored by jailhouse shrinks who classified him as just another malingerer swinging the lead. This assessment changed the moment he plunged a biro pen into Codeye's eyeball with such force it near killed him, the Congolese was certified insane, put into a straightjacket and was last heard barking loudly on his way to Crufts. Codeye blamed the system for losing his eye and bitterness crept into his attitude. He bent the rules, and for a nominal fee would smuggle the odd luxury in. Weekends were particularly tedious; to break the monotony I had Codeye smuggle in a bottle of Vodka. My current position would forbid the renewal of this much valued conduit. A prison governor welcomed me with the news that the barricaders had been busted and the prisoners transhipped to a distant institution. I suggested that the decision to place them on a wing inhabited by predatory monsters wasn't the wisest of moves and a sure recipe for disaster. Unlike the supercilious bigots at Winston Green, the man acknowledged my existence, replying it was only an overnight placement but because of the damage done they had to go. Next time I set eyes upon the barricade brigade was a few days before the trial. Besides myself and Jay there were three other category 'A' residents in the jailhouse, we associated together every afternoon in a cage at the end of the wing. A television was supplied along with board games, packs of cards, half a dozen chairs and a brace of tatty wooden tables completed the décor. Those three were indicted for a particularly gruesome murder which the tabloids sensationalised as 'The Handless Corpse Trial'. Apparently a body, minus its hands and feet, had been discovered by scuba divers ferreting about in a water filled quarry at Chorley. Unfortunately for the intrepid surgical butchers, a gold chain with a unique Chinese symbol was left around the corpse's throat like a birth certificate. This symbol became the subject of a media campaign, a television viewer later identifying the chain as belonging to her missing boyfriend. This revelation sparked an international investigation exposing a drug cartel stretching across the globe. These offenders were in their late twenties to early thirties. Gauging the demeanour, I guessed two of the group were unsuited to criminal intrigue - candidates for promotion hunting police chiefs. I could visualize them being eaten piecemeal by a cabal of ravenous legal vampires.

Errol Hinksman, the third member of the plot, was a native Kiwi, a sophisticated man who had a presence about him. He exuded confidence, spoke several languages and reputedly lived a jet-set lifestyle. He had all the attributes of a lady's man. He had journeyed to the U.K. to visit a friend, Terry Sinclair who was indicted on the handless corpse case and awaiting trial at Wormwood Scrubs prison. Errol was subsequently arrested and charged with murder and a global drug conspiracy along with Sinclair and the two criminal inadequates, a brace of murderers whom he had never met or conversed with before or immediately after the fact. Another illustration of British injustice - the onus being on the accused to prove their incapability or down the tubes they go.

Locked together each afternoon in a human fish tank, two Screws observing bodily interactions and bodily functions, trespassing all over the senses. Paranoia, insecurity, degradation, humiliation, rage, a compendium of neuroses race through the brain before you adapt to such unnatural pressures. Errol endured this microscopic scrutiny for several months prior to our arrival, he welcomed the opportunity to converse with fresh faces. Andy and James, his two co-defendants were criminal debutants inveigled by Sinclair, with a promise of unmeasured prosperity, to slay one of his couriers who had ripped him off. They were both devoid of the necessary cunning or the ruthlessness to perpetrate a cold blooded killing and avoid detection. A calculated act of murder demands the upmost secrecy, an innate ability to retain your own counsel and to share that secrecy with nobody put the participants and the dead man himself. Andy and the naive James involved their respective fiancés in the murderous act by revealing to them their guilt, they voluntarily put a noose around their own necks and were damned to pay the consequences of that evil deed. I intimated that they had more chance of beating the rap if they had tossed the body onto the steps of Scotland Yard with a confession pinned to its chest than telling their spouses.

Apparently it was an open secret in the town they lived in, even the local milkman knew about the slaying and those entangled in the act. The mindless females bragged openly to all and sundry, gushing out the sordid details to the police when they eventually came knocking. A future trial for the two parochial hit-men was pointless, I suggested they plead insanity and throw themselves on the mercy of the courts. My advice was ridiculed, the fools believed that the recriminatory statements would be withdrawn, the legal vampires persuading them to oppose the murder indictment giving the duo false hope. These defence jackals would have represented Adolph Hitler, assuring Adolph that there was nothing for him to worry about, all the evidence was only circumstantial.

An escape strategy was formulated by the two novices and they propositioned me to test my interest. I told them that committing suicide was a safer way of escaping than their ludicrous schemes. One plot involved a gun being secreted at a nominated drop for one of the grassing spouses to bring in on a visit. They had no serious criminal contacts and so they invited me to provide the gun and they would do the rest. I firmly rejected their overtures telling them that I had no interest in joining in any hare-brained schemes and I advised them to take up religion and start praying. It was a tragedy - these two dupes will never see freedom again because of their gullibility and that fate put them in a situation which was way beyond their scope. Errol, on the other hand, had an entirely different persona to the brace of killers, he was cheerful, erudite and optimistic, blessed with organizational skills, and he had ample funds to pay for legal counsel, thereby multiplying his chances of obtaining justice. The case against him was as tenuous as wet tissue paper, based solely on a friendship with Sinclair and a small matter of ten grand in cash which Errol had with him at the time of his arrest. Enough to indict him for murder as far as the authorities were concerned but to win a conviction would take some rigging by the crown. Having no family or friends in the U.K. his only contact with the free world was his legal team and an official from the New Zealand embassy. I connected him to a chatty local maiden who fell head over heels in love with him on the first visit. The girl I was involved with at the time took one cursory glance at Handsome Errol and swiftly tried to do a trade with the local maiden. I established a good rapport with him which lasted many years. Big Fred, a giant of a man, who worked as a bouncer on the doors of some of the

Liverpool night clubs I frequented called out to me one night. I stood at the window which was waist high.

"You ok mate?" Fred boomed loudly across the block from my cell. I homed in on the direction and spotted Big Fred standing at his window.

"Sound Fred. Good to see you mate. What the fuck are you doing in this karsey?" I asked puzzled by his incarceration, he was a legend in club-land with a respected reputation as a hard but fair man, never a criminal though.

"A guy asked me to sit on a parcel of pot. Dropped it off at my place and the next day I'm raided. They find the shit and here I am," he replied, accepting his fate indifferently as a foregone conclusion.

"No way out mate. Hands up and pray you get a decent judge," I said sympathetically, not wanting to go into the politics that the guy who asked him to mind the pot probably set him up. Fred had a line system organised on the block in which we were located. This worked by swinging a line with a pillow case tied on the end containing books for weight and whatever contraband was being passed from cell to cell. Each consecutive cell would grab the line and continue swinging it until it reached its intended destination. Fred made sure I had all the little extras that made jailhouse life a touch easier. A good man, ending up with a four-year penalty for his Good Samaritan portrayal. The laughing policeman visited me on instructions from Fat Sid. He told me that the barricaders' present abode was a prison near Leicester, a jolly old calaboose with friendly staff and an à-la-carte menu. He pumped me to detect any change of heart regarding the spectra of the traitor in our midst. I conveyed my surprise at the man nominated as the Judas who had so conveniently died. It's only in retrospect that these conniving creatures' serpentine scheming became transparent and so blatantly obvious. Ignorance was certainly bliss as far as Fat Sid and his messengers were concerned. If I was aware of the abyss of betrayal that these creatures wallowed in, I certainly wouldn't be exchanging pleasantries with them. In my mind they are condemned to wander endlessly in purgatory for self-serving sins.

"Sid sends his regards. If you need any cash or anything doing, just say the word and it's done," the laughing cop said with a smile stretching across his jaw revealing his pearly white molars. He reminded me of mister Ed, the talking mule.

"What I need is a fuckin' miracle other than that I'm fine," I retorted, still not confident of opening up to this man.

"I don't think Sid can buy one of them," he said, grinning away to himself.

"Any news about the case?" I enquired, seriously changing the mood of the chat. He answered, whispering softly shallow words to placate my worried mind.

"Sid is trying to sort something. He has spoken to someone and there might be a way out. He fixed Vinnie with a top Q.C. from London. He told me to tell you that if anything can be done to help you he will do it."

"Really! Who's he retained for Vinnie – fuckin' Houdini?" I retorted, confused by this snippet of gossip oozing from his laughing lips. Time proved that Fatso did pull a rabbit out of the hat for Vinnie. Mansfield was the Q.C. who conjured up a trick devised by Fatso and his confidantes within law enforcement. He rambled on about influencing a judge to mete out a lenient sentence, a mouthful of verbal excrement delivered on behalf of the sleazy fat man. I never trusted this mule teethed courier. He smiled too much, he also knew too much. An intelligence gatherer linked to Fat Sid - a saboteur of lives. Christmas day in the aquarium was highlighted by the Queen's speech, a facetious toast was proposed by Errol which sparked a row with two Screws who were glued patriotically to the television listening intensely to her every word. The Screws were posted outside the cage; they edged up to the mesh when the Queen began chanting in order to absorb the monarch's words of wisdom.

"Here's to Lizzy, the butcher's apron, the bloodstained empire it flutters over, the poor working class mugs who die penniless on stolen soil," Errol quipped loudly whilst gesturing with a plastic cup in a mock toast. Jed butted in.

"And our lovin' landlady," he laughingly intoned. A rendition of 'To Lizzy' was mouthed by all of us. One of the Screws took offence.

"You Maori shithead. I'd beat your brains in if I heard that kinda talk outside here," he roared angrily at Errol but also glared threateningly at the rest of us. This overt aggressiveness did not go down well.

"Mate, outside here shit like you wouldn't be allowed into the circles I mix in. You pommie tramp," Errol calmly responded to the Screw's barb. This enraged the loyalist who pulled out his baton and smashed the wire mesh viciously in front of Errol, who didn't even flinch at the show of temper. I leapt forward tossing a mug of tea through the steel mesh at the loony loyalist. James picked up a chair crashing it at the mesh, everyone began yelling at the Screw who flapped at this display of unity and dashed to press the alarm bell. A thundering of hooves clattering on the concrete floors heralded the arrival of a posse of reinforcements to assist the hapless chest-beating patriot.

"The bastards have been slagging off the Queen," the flag waver bawled to the breathless mob of Screws, pointing his index finger at us. We were locked inside a steel security cage posing no physical danger to anybody but ourselves. A senior officer took stock of the situation, listened to the squabbling uptight Christmas celebrators, then immediately admonished the two guards and politely asked us to retire to our cells and we duly obliged. The line system supplied us with a steady stream of alcohol and we all got pissed.

New Year's Eve was a party night. Approximately forty cells overlooked a yard; conversing and access to each other posed no problems. Fred organised plenty of booze for the five category 'A' men. He swung a pint of vodka in my direction enabling me to forget, albeit temporarily, the retributive quicksand I had trapped myself in. Big Fred conducted a sing-song as forty drunken criminals stood in front of steel barred windows to welcome in the New Year at H.M.P. Risley. Ali Baba would have been impressed.

A year since the Worcester walloping and still no definite date for a trial, repetition ruled in the fish tank. The two killers received trial depositions showing the case evidence against them which led to a falling out. It appeared that they blamed each other for the dastardly deed in detailed police interviews thus digging deeper the grave in which they were about to be entombed - a prosecutor's delight. A Screw opened me up for exercise and passed a stack of legal hardbacks, a quality dictionary and half a dozen books by Russian authors.

"Hinksman wanted you to have these. Their trial starts tomorrow and they've been moved to the Scrubs," he informed me politely as he gave me the literature. I thanked him for delivering the books. In most jailhouses this gesture would never had happened. The books would have been confiscated then sold on at some local flea market. Because of the bizarre corpse mutilation, Errol's trial had attracted universal media coverage and each day I followed the drama in the newspapers.

Articulate mouthpieces earning their pieces of gold with submissions and objections only served to delay the inevitable guilty verdicts. The sole imponderable to me was the sentencing tariff that the noble judge would eventually impose.

The murder indictment against Errol was not pursued by The Crown, however he was found guilty of money laundering and given the maximum sentence of ten years. An exceedingly steep price to pay for visiting a friend. The two assassins got life imprisonment with a minimum of thirty years, as did the mastermind Sinclair. Andy was unable to cope with this living death sentence and sought refuge in prescribed antidepressant narcotics, turning him into a human vegetable. I met him several years later in H.M.P. Hull; he was a shuffling shell of a man, an ambling cadaver who tottered about talking to himself. I heard that he was later certified insane and transferred to an asylum. Sinclair, who the press alleged had a personal fortune worth in excess of twenty million pounds died in Pankhurst prison of a heart attack. Errol ended up at Long Lartin Prison and was repatriated after six years. James was a native Scot and served his life sentence in the Scottish penal system. The curse of the Chinese symbol inadvertently identified not only the mutilated corpse but sealed the fate of the assassins.

CHAPTER 10

I had a consultation with Wolfe Q.C. regarding the forthcoming trial. Mitigation was the only platform available for him to represent me. I disagreed with his interpretation arguing that evidence of entrapment should be aired in open court forcing the hand of the police into revealing the source of intelligence that led to the Worcester ambush. In short to name the informant. Wolfe was reluctant to pursue this avenue but I was adamant. Early the following morning, a police escort transferred us to Leicester prison wherein we teamed up with the trio of dissident demolishers. I anticipated that our trial was imminent, hence the transfer. A jovial and relatively relaxed atmosphere awaited us in this local prison. A small containment unit catering for just the five of us, manned by non-confrontational Screws, was to be our base for the trial. Arrangements to have suits and ties for courtroom protocol was made by the authorities. Billy, who decided to defend himself, requested black silks befitting his self-acclaimed barrister status. This inane request was rejected despite Billy's long-winded, tongue-in-cheek protestations. The trial was staged at Worcester Shire Court. A judge with all kinds of medieval titles, including the Sherriff of Worcestershire was the nominated adjudicator for the case. A brief word with counsel took place in the underground cells before we ascended into a Cromwellian setting that was a sight to behold. An historic chamber filled with dignitaries that I thought belonged to the pages of history books. The Shires had done itself proud, folk wearing admirals uniforms adorned with rows of medals and campaign ribbons, Army Field Marshals dressed to kill, wives of these V.I.P.s attired in flowing gowns and swanky bonnets. A number of these anachronistic throwbacks wore ceremonial swords. It was as if we had entered a time capsule and landed in the middle ages. The ostentatious pomp climaxed with the Lord High Sherriff, the judge, escorted to the judicial throne by two sword carrying valets wearing bright coloured beefeater costumes. He sat down to a declaration of his name and a list of titles bestowed upon him. Glancing at the ermine robe and the buckled shoes I wondered if he played Old King Cole at the Christmas pantomimes. A puritan looking clerk read out our names and the indictment, we each responded with a not guilty plea. Legal submissions were made on our behalf and an interlude was agreed whereupon due process and the rule of law could be debated. In my mind this was legal jiggery-pokery, a game of charades. We retired to the cells whilst the dignitaries and the cluster of legal minds retired to anterooms and a glass of claret.

"What the fuck is going on here. Half the armed forces are on the plot," Billy declared, a bit concerned by the excessive theatricals in the court. "Never seen so many fuckin' medals. It's a wonder the Pope isn't here," Jay chipped in sarcastically.

"What's going on here mate is a fuckin' show trial. These bastards are gonna crucify us," I stated emphatically. This was no ordinary sessions this was a kangaroo court set up to throw the proverbial book at us.

"What happens, fuckin' happens," Vinnie contributed philosophically.

"Maybe, but let's make sure it doesn't happen here. I've a funny feeling about this bollocks, these bastards will hammer us." I contended a feeling of apprehension creeping into my consciousness.

"I'm fighting this all the way. I'm pleading guilty to fuck-all," Billy recited stubbornly, determined to stave of the inevitable jail sentence.

"Let's see what shit the briefs come back with," suggested Jay who still believed in fairy tales.

"Fuck all! They'll come back with fuck-all. The prosecution will offer to drop the conspiracy charge if we plead guilty to the robbery. If this happens, don't accept it. This is a fuckin' ploy for the fancy dress brigade in the courthouse. The shower of slags will have a party sorted," I ranted, convinced that we were lambs about to be slaughtered.

"I fuckin' agree with you mate. That's why I'm defending myself to support my suspicions.

Jon who never spoke just nodded his head approvingly, Jay understood this was smelling of a carve-up, Vinnie implied he wanted to get it over and done with. After lunch a procession of Silks and solicitors gathered in a large holding cell to debate a procedural development. Plead guilty to the robbery at Worcester and the Conspiracy indictment would be dropped. I anticipated this move, it was nigh impossible to proceed with the conspiracy charge because the C.P.S. and the police had cocked it up by not checking the fact that I was incarcerated on two counts, Billy was in custody on another. Wolfe brought this to the notice of the prosecution who had no choice but to drop the entire conspiracy allegations. What concerned me was a guilty plea in front of these medieval piranhas. There was no doubt in my mind that if capital punishment was an option, this court would hang us by the neck until dead. Accepting the plea bargain offered by an eager Crown Prosecutor today would prove disastrous. Not according to all the honourable defence lawyers who used their considerable powers of persuasion to talk us into accepting the proposal. The purity of soul dispensed by these paragons of untainted virtue would have shamed the archangel Gabriel, such was the sanctimonious diatribe resorted to in an effort to convince us to plead guilty. Needless to say we rejected their supplications and elected to stand trial. Wolfe was distraught.

"Mr. Smith - it's inconceivable for me to mount a defence on your behalf. Your stance is absurd," Wolfe declared with obvious annoyance.

A similar dialogue was being pursued by his black-gowned colleagues.

"I'm innocent, the only thing I'm guilty of is posting a letter and being ambushed by gun slinging police officers," I lied purposely intimating to him that there's little prospect of me accepting the offer of a guilty before this parody of the Spanish Inquisition. He sighed loudly with frustration, his patience sinking into his well-heeled boots.

"You were apprehended at the scene of the crime, shot by an officer of the law, identified by a postman and half a dozen police officers, you wore a balaclava, the evidence against you is irrefutable. It is my duty to advise you to accept the prosecution's offer," he decreed with an air of finality.

I ignored his analysis and legal supposition.

"Circumstances may indicate that I'm guilty but I assure you I'm not. I most emphatically deny the allegations against me and demand a jury trial," I said defensively, staring coldly into his eyes for several seconds. I was not prepared to play ball with this society of Freemasonry.

"You are a fool," he concluded, shaking his bewigged head sadly.

"Maybe so, but I refuse to kowtow to that gaggle of fancy dressed peacocks. I'll take my chances with a jury of my peers," I declared anxious to postpone today's date with the inquisitors.

Each of my fellow conspirators replicated my position, electing to go for trial. Five disgruntled legal falcons were subsequently discharged of their services. We were led back into the dock; the assemblage of costumed aristocrats all squatted in rank, the Lord High Sheriff's frustration engraved like an epitaph across his furrowed brow gave us a withering look, we had outflanked the partygoers and spoilt their celebratory ball. We were remanded for trial on the robbery count to a future date allowing us time to appoint fresh counsel. I decided to refrain from the charade and defend myself. One of the solicitors popped in to see us prior to us being shunted back to prison. He had an earhole connection to the judge's chambers and confirmed what we had already suspected - we were about to be sacrificed on the High Sheriff's judicial altar. He detailed the sentences that would have been imposed, which far exceeded the tariff befitting the crime. I would have received a life sentence form the Shire Sheriff, the very epitome of justice. Fuck' em!

Two months rapidly passed. Vinnie's legal team petitioned for a change of venue away from the Worcester cowsheds on the basis that the undue publicity would prejudice a fair and just trial. Thankfully the motion was granted and we were arraigned at Birmingham Crown Court under the stewardship of Justice Mais, the sleeping man. He couldn't keep his eyes open and constantly nodded off as if he was doped up with Valium. At one stage of the proceedings I thought he had died. He would have been more at home on a mortuary slab than semi-comatose on a judicial throne. He appeared to be in his eighties, brittle boned, with sunken eye sockets and his skin taut on his porcelain snow-white face. The Brummies named him the battery operated judge. A conference cell guarded by armed police was available to us in the depths of the court. After we had appeared and answered to the indictment, an adjournment was agreed by both sides for some legal horse trading. I requested an explanation about the rules of disclosure before I would participate in any legal rituals. I was attempting to pressure the prosecution into revealing the source of the intelligence that led to the ambush. This was a strategy to support evidence of entrapment and police complicity in a crime. Something for the opposition to contemplate in the subsequent horse trading stakes. Police protected at all costs their undercover plants.

Instead of a drawn-out trial, a deal was proposed that a guilty plea would be viewed favourably by the court. Billy, who was representing himself asked what the sentence would be if we accepted this proposal. A messenger contacted a Crown official who refused to be specific on the issue of sentencing. I rejected the proposal, counteracting with an offer to plead guilty to the lesser count of burglary, otherwise I will go to trial. Once the others heard the baseless, ludicrous concession I put to the Crown they swiftly jumped on the burglary bandwagon. Jon's barrister pleaded with me to speak to the muted, antisocial Jon who had refused to converse or acknowledge the barrister's role in defending him.

"Listen mate - you need to chat with this guy. He's here to help you," I softly advised the reclusive Jon.

He was sitting alone in a corner of the large conference cell. At this moment the cell was crowded with solicitors and bewigged barristers. Stanley was three metres away staring on furtively.

"I'm not havin' that ugly bastard speakin' for me. He looks like Ben Turpin, the googled eyed scruffbag," the normally reticent Jon snarled then turned to stare at the wall.

"Don't be silly mate. Just feed him a load of bollocks. Ok?" I tried to cajole him into cooperating with this legal leper.

Stanley stood isolated from the hectic debating rattling around the cell, puffing away on a seemingly endless supply of cigarettes. I felt a moment of pity for him. Jon carried on staring at the wall.

Vinnie's Q.C., the esteemed and much lauded Michael

Mansfield, conducted the wrangling, listening to a reel of critical castigations of the police ambush, disclosure of the grass, mitigation bullshit, a futile guilty to a simple burglary count, before his battered ears had suffered enough. He called time out. He departed with three other barristers to attend a meeting with the prosecution to finalize our future. A supply of food was delivered as we awaited the return of the emissaries. An air of high-velocity tension enveloped us all. The end-game was about to commence, clammy hands and periods of silence replaced the humorous banter. Accepting responsibility for a crime wasn't an issue, the consequences of a robbery was a gamble we were all well aware of. The penalty varied from hope to hopelessness; that was the concern we had as we waited in the throes of limbo. A discordant symphony of jingle jangling keys alerted us to the arrival of the envoys; we got to our feet and braced ourselves for the deal on the table. Resembling the four horsemen of the apocalypse, the four black robed, sombre faced advocates trotted purposefully into the dull dank dungeon and delivered the Crown's final offer or we go to trial. Mansfield addressed the floor. He announced firmly to the five of us...

"I have persuaded the prosecution to communicate with the judge that you will all plead guilty with the proviso that there will be a ceiling on the sentences imposed."

"What may I ask is this proposed ceiling?" I enquired, suspicion burrowing its way into my thought process.

"Twelve years is the maximum figure agreed upon," he decreed confidently and scrutinised our faces for a reaction.

I shook my head, ruminating the offer whilst analysing the alternatives. Billy enquired if they would put it in writing. Vinnie had a quick whispering session with Mansfield, Jay shrugged his shoulders whilst Jon kept on staring at the wall ignoring everything. We asked for a few minutes privacy whilst we run through the trade-off. After a brief period of bartering a written declaration was requested affirming the sentencing but this was deemed to be improbable. A compromise was reached with Mansfield giving his word that nobody would receive a prison sentence in excess of twelve years. Handshakes were exchanged as the quartet of briefs departed and prepared for court. The rainbow hues of the packed courtroom gave a surrealistic feeling to the events ahead. It felt as if I was treading through a fog-bound muddy clogged bog. I inhaled deeply to clear my head allowing oxygen to erase the mist and restore some clarity to my consciousness. We lined up in the dock flanked by Screws and Mad Mannering's tactical mob. A roll-call of our names were announced followed by a barely audible and reluctant guilty plea. Mannering stared across the court at me, a smirk splitting his oily face, he gestured with his hand as if he was pointing a pistol to his head, simultaneously mouthing 'you're getting fucked now'. I immediately leapt to my feet and challenged him to repeat the threat. This created a shouting match resulting in the judge dismissing Mannering from the court room. He was furious. We all remained seated whilst each of the legal team spouted pleas of mitigation on behalf of their respective clients. Vinnie's brief painted a fabricated portrayal of his charity work, his devotion to the deprived and starving orphans of Uganda, testimonies of his care for the elderly in the community. Listening to this embellishment of reality made me wonder if I'd been nicked with one of Christ's disciples instead of a career criminal. Jay's counsel depicted him as a lost soul who drifted into crime because of a severely deprived background; he was one of fourteen children who lived like sardines in a three bedroom slum. Five of his siblings shared the same bed with him and he had wandered the streets searching for scraps of food from the age of four. I didn't know whether to laugh or cry at this plea for mercy. Stanley testified to Jon's frailties, devoid of any background ammunition about him because he never exchanged one word. Billy was a career criminal; he was cast as an unfortunate bit player who got involved at the last minute; he thought he was going on a burglary not an armed robbery. A child of the Liverpool slums who was led astray by others into a regrettable life of crime. He was truly remorseful for his actions and promised to lead an honest life if the court saw fit to give him one more chance. A heart rending plea was concluded by Billy's counsel.

Justice Mais slept throughout these elaborate pastiches. He was so old that he had more than likely heard every fabricated extenuation tale in the book. The dice had already been rolled, the cadre of briefs were going through the motions, earning their corn with stage managed pointless theatrics. I was asked if I had anything to say before sentencing and I responded with a curt "nothing to say."

The judge roused from his slumber, an aide offered him a glass of water which he sipped peckishly as he peeped slyly at us like a vulture about to devour a helpless wounded animal. He addressed us individually espousing the usual clichés about gambling for high stakes and losing. Jay, Jon, and Vinnie were each given nine years, Billy was sentenced to twelve years imprisonment. He singled me out and gushed forth with a torrent of abuse.

"Smith, you are an intelligent man who has deliberately chosen a criminal lifestyle. You are prepared to use extreme violence to achieve your goals. I have a duty to protect the public from you and your kind. You will go to prison for twelve years." He spoke coldly and emphatically - the contempt dripping from his silver tongue. A human specimen who would never suffer from a crisis of conscience. I wasn't too perturbed by this sentence, it could have been far worse. I gazed at this semi-comatose, half dead privileged aristocrat, mirroring the contemptuous vibes radiating from his decrepit body. I momentarily lost my cool...

"Thank you. I will be free to walk about this courtroom in seven years' time, whereas you, you cliché riddled bag of bones will be fuckin' dead. I'll piss on your grave," I bawled out loudly at him as the Screws dragged me out of the dock. The dithering pensioner didn't hear one word of what I had hurled at him. He was exhausted from staying awake long enough to fulfil his sentencing duty. I was guided back to the underground dungeon. Vinnie was overjoyed at the nine year penalty, he had expected much longer. I was somewhat confused at the three years disparity in the sentences. There was no criminal virgins amongst us and each of us had served prison terms before this event - nobody had cooperated with the police for a reduction in jail time. Who had devised and advised the Crown to dispense justice by apportioning blame in such discriminatory fashion took some analysis over the years. I managed to prove that the disparity was unjust in law but failed to get a reduction from a Lord Chief Justice who waved a legal wand dismissing my appeal based on an ancient bylaw dating from the Magna Carta. I was immediately ghosted from the court on my own to be subsequently dumped in Wormwood Scrubs prison. One of Britain's most overcrowded stinking human warehouses.

CHAPTER 11

Wormwood Scrubs, a Dickensian style workhouse teeming with social misfits, petty offenders and mental inadequates. A bustling hive of activity complimented by a ceaseless buzz of voices. The jail seemed to have a life of its own; it felt like I was travelling through the internal organs of some gigantic beast. I was delivered into the reception area, showered and given prison-issue clothes, the trousers and jacket embossed with broad yellow stripes, denoting my category 'A' status. I was escorted to a solitary cell bearing a board with a black letter 'A' painted on it. A large cardboard box was passed to me by a guard.

"Put all of your clothing, including shoes, into the box it will be collected each night at suppertime, make sure you're stripped to your pyjamas." A Screw with a belly like a pregnant female about to give birth to triplets barked out at me. I cast a cursory glance at him and strode into this concrete tomb and tossed my meagre possessions onto a rusty bed frame upon which rested a piss stained mattress.

"The recess is over there," he pointed to an alcove about twenty metres along the landing, "Hurry up and get yourself some water," he recited this as if he were doing me a great favour.

I quickly picked up two large plastic water jugs and strode over to the urine scented recess with the obese Screw waddling behind me. I filled up and returned to my cell with the blubbery anthropological shire-horse struggling to keep pace with me. The door slammed and I was left to reflect upon the mistakes I had made that had plunged me into this subliminal vortex for the next seven years or so. An alien environment, wherein the libido is castrated, heterosexual relationships repressed and consigned to the depths of the subconscious, normality discarded and self-discipline the panacea for survival. A just punishment perhaps, but increased tenfold by the socially inadequate, the mental defectives, and the innumerable lunatics that infest the penal gulags like a malignant tumour. These nutters would demolish the mental equilibrium of a temple packed with Buddhist monks.

After breakfast a ferret-faced Screw poked his scrawny neck inside the cell door and asked me if I wished to go to a workshop for a couple of hours each morning sewing mailbags and I nodded in the affirmative. The alternative was to remain banged up. Shortly thereafter two mute androids opened my door and beckoned me to follow them. I was escorted to a single story factory humming with convicts slaving away on sewing machines where they delivered me to a security Screw perched on a raised podium. A log-book containing my photograph was passed to the security officer who duly signed it.

"Right Smith, sit next to him," he ordered gruffly, pointing to a row of chairs approximately four metres in front of the podium. I shuffled across and squatted down. There were two rows of six chairs upon which sat ten or so category 'A' prisoners sewing mailbags by hand. A boot-licking faggot sidled up to me bearing a sheet of Hessian, a ball of twine and a steel needle. The trustee then demonstrated the technical aspects of needlework. I gave him a scornful look and sent him on his way with an earful of profanities. The chair area was taboo for the mainstream prisoners who were not allowed to mingle near us on security grounds. A load of bollocks but that was how the system functioned in these allocation centres. The guy I sat next to introduced himself...

"I'm Dicky this is my Mate Bobby," he said in a soft Belfast accent. I reciprocated the gesture and offered them my hand. He was a distinguished looking man in his mid-forties, tall and of medium build, his eyes were steely blue and he had a presence about him. Bobby, his compatriot, was a bit younger, stockily built and his face bore the scars of a troubled and violent past. He had an overtly aggressive disposition. They were both Republican prisoners, both incarcerated for a conspiracy to hijack a helicopter in an attempt to further the escape of I.R.A. prisoners by forcing the hijacked helicopter down onto the exercise yard of a maximum-security institution. Unfortunately they were intercepted by the Special Branch on the way to the helicopter pad, arrested, and as a consequence forfeited their liberty.

"Wasn't you the Scouser that got shot by the Peelers?" enquired Dicky as he fumbled about with the finer details of needlework.

"The pricks used me for target practice. They thought I was a fuckin' clay pigeon mate," I answered cynically.

"Bastards, did you see Hughie Dougherty after he was done?" interjected Bobby inquisitively. This subtle interrogation process was to establish my bona fides. I later discovered that the sewing circle duo were prominent members of the Republican movement and as such they were wary of speaking to strangers in case they were plants. Paranoia was an essential tool in the jail house survival kit of long-term residents. Within the claustrophobic high razor-wired walls lurks soulless desperados, who seek premature release by bartering the lives of their friends, cell mates, mothers and anything or anybody that may unlock the main gates to freedom.

"We was behind the door when the Screws kicked the fucking shit out of him. A gang of fuck pigs up there," I responded to the query, fully aware of their innate suspicions.

"I heard that a Scouse firm stood by him, thanks mate," Dicky retorted satisfied that I wasn't a government agent. Bobby the simmering volcano still had reservations.

On a previous stint trekking across the gulags, I encountered numerous I.R.A. captives with whom I trained in the gym. They were a tight lipped group who never discussed their offences nor any machinations of their organization. One who I was familiar with was Billy Armstrong, who was serving a monumental term of natural life. He hailed from the Falls Road area of Belfast, the same area as the two hijackers, they both knew him well. This snippet of gossip broke the ice enabling the volcanic Bobby to relax.

"How's the food in this pisshole?" I enquired, the pangs of hunger for ever pushing to the forefront of my brain.

"Fuckin' steamed shite. A pig would turn its snout up to the offal dished up here," barked Bobby, his simmering fury rising to the surface.

"Ignore him, Tom... the grub's edible but the portions are paltry. Bobby would complain if he got fillet steak every day," spouted Dicky diplomatically. The antagonistic Bobby responded with a curt expletive. He wanted to bomb the prison kitchen.

Food was high on the agenda of penal priorities, it not only nourishes the body and pacifies the spirit it also influences attitude and behaviour patterns. Poor food is often the catalyst for riots and violent outbursts. Monday to Friday the sewing circle mornings turned into a debating society whereby the three of us engaged in dissecting the political ideology of the World. Thatcherism was at its zenith, the iron maiden was riding high on the back of the Falklands fiasco. Media outlets glorified her exploits as she pranced about, handbag clutched to her hip, spewing jingoistic colonial guff to a fawning public. A celestial star who exuded an imperious arrogance that belied her humble origins as a grocer's daughter. Rumour around the cell blocks was that Thatcher was planning to usurp the Monarchy, exiling the Germanic Windsors to the Falklands thereby crowning herself the Queen of England. She certainly had the pompous emotional aloofness that befits a monarch. The Irishmen considered her the epitome of evil, an enemy of Ireland and the scourge of the working classes.

Night-time in the cell block was a particularly gruelling occasion; it resembled a menagerie alive with squawking rabid creatures. Hundreds of short-term felons caged in the tiers above me would start screeching and cackling out of the barred windows to each other as they negotiated contraband deals. A crude line system would be operating continuously as the noise-making cabbages swung the parcels from one end of the block to the other. This ordeal began at seven-thirty every night until it ceased at ten p.m. when the lights were switched off causing a mass blanket of silence to descend over the cell blocks.

During this period a couple of bombs exploded in the centre of London inducing a feeling of outrage towards the Irish Republican insurgents. The first device was in Hyde Park, which detonated during a daily cavalry march past to Horse Guards Parade. A bomb hidden inside a car exploded, windows shattered for miles around, flames burst high into the sky, horses fell in a writhing mass, their bodies ripped to shreds, dying soldiers' shrieks of agony pierced the air, the urban street resembled a scene from a battlefield. Many soldiers and horses died and countless more were injured.

A couple of hours later on a bandstand in Regents Park, the regimental band of The Green Jackets was giving a concert. As the band struck up a tune, a bomb secreted under the stage exploded and the entire bandstand erupted scattering bodies and instruments high into the air. Men died, men screamed, blood and limbs incongruously stained the grassland of this public park. In one bloody day the I.R.A. had brought the war against England to the doorsteps of the English nation. The Thatcher Junta continued to plough the fields of Britain with patriotic optimism and intransigence.

I listened on the radio in my cell to news bulletins about the bombings. A horse named Sefton that was mutilated by the blast, figured prominently in the reports. Pictures of the horse blood streaming from its wounds was on the front pages of all the daily newspapers. A captain of the Horse Guards was seen stuffing his shirt into a hole in the horse's body to stem the flow of blood. Sefton eventually recovered from the shrapnel trauma going on to become a national hero, receiving awards for bravery, opening fetes and supermarkets, making personal appearances at major sporting events. It captured the hearts of a nation.

That night the faceless window gossip mongers ranted and raved anti-Irish sentiments to each other. Some of the petty offenders, probably in for non-payment of a gas bill, were singing old colonial anthems to each other whilst their kids were starving outside struggling on their way to school with holes in their worn out second hand shoes. My cell door was opened the following morning by the blubbery waddle-walking Screw.

"Smith, you ok for the shop today," he requested, a touch of concern added to his tone.

"I'm sound mate. What's the problem?" I replied, aware of the hostility drummed up by the window gossipers.

"No problem. If you're happy with the Irish bastards," he snarled, glaring at me with contempt.

"I'd rather identify with them than a windbag like you fatty," I quipped, mirroring his animosity. He slammed the door after calling me a Scouse prick.

Two mutants collected me and escorted me to the workshop.

As I made my way towards the sewing circle it felt as if hundreds of eyes were firing laser beams at the two Irishmen. The tension was stifling, clouding the air like a dense fog. I touched base and picked up the embroidery tackle and greeted the two unperturbed Republicans.

"It fuckin' feels like the Brits are gonna nail us to a fuckin' cross chaps," growled Bobby loudly as he flexed his broad shoulders, turned and took in the antipathy sizzling away amongst the restless pack of mailbag stitchers.

"Blank them mate. They're fuckin' sheep looking for a shepherd," I interjected, hoping to take the sting out of the situation.

"Tomorrow these guys will be more concerned about their visitors being late than having a ruckus with us," Dicky stated calmly to the hyperactive Bobby. The fickleness of human nature accompanied by a herd mentality was an observation understood by the astute Irishman.

"Fuck 'em," Blurted the apathetic Bobby.

A voiced suddenly yelled loudly, "you fucking murderous Irish scumbags, killing defenceless horses." A wave of dissenting muttering swept the shop-floor towards us. Bobby slowly rose to his feet and turned to a cockney bank robber.

"What did you fuckin' say, arsehole?" He bellowed aggressively, letting him know that he wouldn't be intimidated by anyone.

George, the bank robber wasn't the culprit who shouted out the slanderous slur but nevertheless he took umbrage.

"I said fuck-all Paddy but I'm no fuckin' arsehole. Cunt," George retorted his hackles up. He then slung a mail bag forcefully at Bobby's face.

Bobby brushed it to one side, leapt forward and landed a haymaker on George's jaw rendering him unconscious. A free-for-all ensued with punches, kicks, head-butts, wrestling holds being exchanged between us three pariahs and the rest of the sewing circle group. The Screw on the pulpit hit the alarm bell then scurried off to the staff toilet seeking sanctuary. The doors burst open letting in a tribe of whooping, baton-wielding Screws who were already on standby prepared for trouble. They stampeded through the shop like a band of Apaches looking for a scalp manhandling anyone who stood in their path. A machinist shouted loudly, "watch out lads, here comes the fuckin' keystone cops."

A Screw flew at the wisecracking machinist beating him about the head and shoulders with a cosh, blood spilling all over his face and turning his prison shirt bright red. For this sinner, not only did crime not pay but humour paid far less.

As the chanting war party approached swinging their batons, hostilities ceased as we considered that discretion was the best part of valour. We were herded into a corner of the shop by the breathless mob of chest-beating pit bulls who had to be restrained by a senior officer from steaming in to give us a good thrashing. Peace restored, two chest-beaters proceeded to escort us individually back to our cells where they instructed us that it was the end of the daily sewing circle sessions, reverting back to one hour of exercise each day.

Long term gulag inhabitants couldn't give a damn about the Queen and country jingoism or for utterings spewed by unscrupulous, patriotic flag waving, money grabbing politicians. A totally different calibre of personnel haunt these institutions; the minimum sentence was five years with the majority of the residents serving indeterminate terms of ten years to life. Sectarianism was a concept foreign to this society; the reactions to the bombing campaigns would be opposite to that displayed by the decomposing scruff-bags at the Scrubs. The Irish contingent were accepted and respected.

The emissary of Foxy Fat Sid, the laughing policeman turned

up on a visit bearing greetings from his deceitful mentor. His mission to surreptitiously extract intelligence about the plot that jailed us and to discover if I nurtured any suspicions as to Fatso's role in my downfall. I look back in anger at the gullible head that sat on my shoulders during this stage of my life, being outwitted by these devious miscreants bemuses me to this day. Sid slept on pillows of paranoia and used emissaries as life preservers in the event that his undercover police work might be exposed, giving the lump of lard time to take the necessary steps to protect his duplicity.

A large wooden shed sufficed as a visiting room. A dozen or so Formica topped tables dotted the interior, four tatty wooden chairs parked by each, a hatch at the rear of the shed served tea and coffee. As I squatted on the rickety chair the laughing cop slithered in, a smirk stretched across his lower jaw as wide as the River Mersey. I looked at the donkey-toothed, smiling creep as he placed a plastic cup of watery coffee opposite me, wondering what brought him on the long journey from Liverpool to the capital city. Having dispensed with the small talk, the giggling goon brought the meeting around to the real reason for his trip.

"What about the other grassing bastard getting killed in a crash? Un-fuckin'-believable mate," he stated emphatically, shaking his equine head in a show of incredulity.

"Fuckin' amazing. I couldn't understand it when I heard that he'd blew us up," I replied, accepting the revelation that the death of the nominated grass and his wife was true at the time. I don't think old donkey teeth was aware at this point that anybody, other than the car crash victim, was the guilty party. He was just a mere errand boy.

"All the chaps are fuckin' shocked. If he fuckin' pawned people he deserved to die. Fuckin' prick," exclaimed the messenger boy assessing my opinion on the subject

"A first class prick. Fucking deserves his place in Hell," I responded to his castigation of a poor man wrongly damned for something he never done.

A number of topics were covered about the fate of the rest of the Worcester gang; where they had relocated to and the fact that Fatso was taking care of their welfare. I soon became bored of his gossiping guff, curtailed the visit, bade him farewell and returned to my cell.

I exercised on my own for the next week or so, a smug faced Screw informed me that both of the Irish chaps had been ousted to other prison camps and that I will be kicked out in the not too distant future. I ignored his comments marching around in circles lost in the many landscapes stored within my mind.

Six a.m. next day, a group of long coated warders opened my cell ordering me to get dressed forthwith as I was being transhipped to fresh pastures. They were a sombre bunch with the air of an executioner, lingering grim-faced as I swilled my face and put on my prison rags. I was swiftly ushered through the prison gates where I was placed in a van and driven out to be joined by an armed police escort. I asked one of the poker faced Screws were I was going. He refused to declare our destination as if he were on a secret service mission. I told him to fuck off.

CHAPTER 12

As the prison van halted in front of the huge reinforced prison gates, I took a hard look at the free world, taking in the passing traffic, the odd carefree pedestrian and the armed police who had escorted the van to this penal mausoleum. A sight that became a memory embedded on the frontal lobe for the next six or seven years. The attitude displayed by Hull's custodians was cordial and devoid of the overt antipathy that clouded the thick skulls of the transit-camp staff. Hull presented a far more relaxed regime that combined a virtually escape-proof perimeter with a less restricted society inside the prison.

I was met in the reception area by a smiling jovial Screw who introduced himself as Officer Black; he informed me of what privileges I was allowed under Hull's liberal policies of reform and rehabilitation. A euphemism for toe the line otherwise you'll get fuck-all and tossed back into the transit sewage system.

"As you're staying with us for a long time, Scouse, you can have curtains, a rug and bedspread, a record player, training gear for the gym, a budgie and cage, all sent in from your family or friends," he chirped off, parrot fashion like a latter day Samaritan chatting to a suicidal caller.

"Any chance of conjugal visits then?" I asked bluntly as the Samaritan fumbled with his welcoming list. He returned my sarcasm with a smirk.

"I'm afraid that stage of liberalism hasn't quite reached us yet, Scouse, maybe in the not too distant future, some Home Secretary will bring it in," he responded sincerely, believing his own bullshit.

"They're all fuckin' faggots. Most of them have marriages of convenience.

They'd hang you from the gallows before agreeing to a conjugal visit," I blurted out cynically to the overtly polite day-dreaming warder.

"Scouse, take it easy, I'm with you. I'm only employed by the government. I don't care for some of the policies and procedures but there's nothing I can do about it," he replied passively, misinterpreting my statement as inflammatory and confrontational. I was expressing my contempt for political ministers and their blatant hypocrisy. I had no intention of locking horns with the conscientious Officer Black. A humble civil servant doing his duty unlike the thugs that patrolled the tiers of the karseys I'd been banged up in the past two years or so.

Black escorted me from reception to a cell on A-wing which would be a temporary base until I went through a ritual induction process. A round of mind games to assess what work was suitable and what wing I would be allocated to for the duration of my detention. My status as an A-listed prisoner did not affect me at all in this establishment; most of the clientele were either on the A-list or had recently been downgraded, I had as much freedom of movement as the next man. Approximately two-fifths of the five hundred inmates were serving life sentences for murder, the rest being made up of armed robbers, gangsters, violence merchants, kidnappers, terrorists, burglars and the odd drug dealer. Drugs hadn't yet exploded onto the streets turning council estates into wastelands filled with junkies and providing massive wealth for the importers and the dealers.

Thatcher's decimation of the working-class industrial heartland and the slow strangulation of working-men's souls paved the way for a generation existing on benefits and living in council slums. A cannabis coma subculture mushroomed in these deprived areas providing the occupants a refuge from the reality of unemployed despair and endless tedium. Pride vanquished, sacrificed upon the altar of ill-conceived economic madness. Dealing and using drugs became the norm on council estates the length and breadth of the nation.

Arthur Scargill, a truly noble man, was put to the sword by the merciless and vindictive grocer's daughter, who bribed the police to attack and crush the spirit of Arthur and his union supporters. Opportunities to earn a decent living became as rare as the dodo. This bitter defeat terminated the right for a man to work for a living and to be paid a decent wage. Successive generations never had any work experience, drugs became the pivotal axis of estate society, life revolved around the economy provided by drugs.

There were maybe twenty people in Hull for drug related offences when I was incarcerated there in 1982. Today the prison population has more than doubled and ninety percent of those convicted are in for drugs, or crimes originating from the narcotic trade. Assigning blame is never straightforward but if prison is a reflection of our society, then the fact that today's jails are jam-packed with the products of the council estates points to the insufferable profiteering pursued by the Tory brigands under the mantle of Thespian Thatcher. Instead of bestowing titles and Peerages or building statues to these fortune hunting bounders, these corrosive political criminals, effigies of them should be burning in the streets, their stiffs should be hanging from lamp-posts. More damage has been inflicted upon urban England by this firm of charlatans than Hitler's Luftwaffe.

After officer Black departed leaving the cell door unlocked, I unpacked my few belongings then proceeded to make up a bed; my reverie was interrupted by a booming voice calling out my name. I strode out of the cell taking a peek in the direction of the commotion. A ghost from the past was at the wing office staring up at me, a broad grin lighting up his face. It was Delroy, a long standing neighbourhood friend who evolved from the same streets as me. A power-house, huge biceps, a well-built body builder who chose to pursue a career of crime and had spent a big chunk of his life being persecuted for his misdeeds, wallowing in a multiplicity of penal pits. A friendly face uplifted my spirits. Delroy shouted my name then raced up the stairwell to greet me. He carried a bag containing a jar of coffee, tea, milk, biscuits and a mixture of toiletries which he had brought for me. At the end of each tier was a hot water urn, I quickly used the facility to enjoy my first cup of strong coffee for two years.

"What have the barbaric bastards done to you my friend?" Delroy enquired as he took stock of the state of my traumatised arm. He was articulate, bore no trace of a Liverpool accent and was well read with a virtual library of literary quotations. A paradoxical trait as he had a fearsome reputation with a great capacity for violence.

"The Old Bill tried to whack me. Lucky the guy had fuckin' jelly flowing through his veins otherwise I'd have been a dead man. I'll get myself in the gym and build up the muscle," I replied, showing him the battle scar tissue. To meet up with this raconteur who was good entertainment and a never-ending catalogue of tales was a most welcoming relief.

"Fools who blindly perform their duty devoid of the moral courage to question the authority that orders them to slay their fellow Christians. Fear, not God will judge these philistines," he preached with an enormous grin on his face, he acted the part of a Bible-bashing believer. A man with a myriad of complex personalities that surfaced to the fore according to whichever particular doctrine he was studying at the time. I assumed he was on a religious kick.

"Fuck the philistines and fuck God. What's the chance of having it away from this pisshole." I declared curious to discover if he had spotted any weaknesses in this fortress's impregnability. Escape was a notion I had juggled with since my arrest.

"State of the art security technology; cameras poking up your rectum, tremblers on the internal fencing, twenty-four hour dog patrol, escape-proof I would conclude," he replied, obviously having looked at the possibility of busting free.

A decade or so later he escaped from a European jail with the aid of a helicopter and outside assistance. It made international headlines.

"In transit is the only way out then. No fuckin' chance on this A-list bollocks," I sighed, resigned to serve out the full tariff imposed by the courts. If I had not been classified as a security risk, I'm sure I would have squeezed through the steel bars and made good my bid for freedom before I ever got to the trial stages. Devoid of a security status, escaping from the local transit camps was easily accomplished in those days, I had previously slipped away from custody, as had associates of mine. Accepting my current situation meant taking each day as it came and making the best use of the years entombed in this pyramidal sarcophagus.

Hull's internal social structure was a galaxy removed from the Wandsworth and the Winston Greens coercive compost heaps. Dialogue was encouraged between the staff and the residents and confrontational situations were avoided by the custodians. In a claustrophobic, containment society populated by psychopaths with nothing to lose, men who had perpetrated an encyclopaedia of heinous crimes, such as matricide, patricide, pyromania and necrophilia mingled with men who had slaughtered their wives and fiancées, beheaded their lovers and butchered their neighbours in fits of madness.

Subjecting this bunch of pacifists to an intimidatory regime would end in carnage. Co-existence was dependent upon mutual cooperation and an element of respect. Hull epitomised this aspect of penology, doing 'time' was relatively easy if you played the game.

Most of the killers were now institutional men, left alone to mutate in satellite communities that had formed within the different prison cell blocks. They have adapted to the prospect that their only exit will be as a cadaver inside a coffin carted to an unknown penal burial site. A subculture fermenting in the shadows of the mainstream convict society, they're like ghosts floating about with blank expressions on their ashen faces, lifers living in a fungal web devoid of sunlight, death an embraceable salvation for this parade of zombies.

The induction period took three days of interviews with a mixed bag of profilers before they assessed a work plan and wing location suitable for me. This was an era of infinite stupidity when the rehabilitation sociologists held a belief that hard-core recidivists could be transformed into choirboys. Career criminals with a modicum of intellect mastered their own destiny, a quorum of psychology professors with all the analytical data available would ultimately fail to persuade any of the robbers I mingled with to go straight. Age was what rehabilitated criminals not university graduates perusing text books and then regurgitating empirical bullshit.

I was allocated to C-wing, declared fit for light duties, assigned to an educational degree course at the prison in-house college. This precluded me from slaving away in the jail's manufacturing base where most of the inhabitants occupied themselves producing furniture and steel beds for other establishments. There was also a large laundry that took in the bedding and towels from N.H.S. Hospitals in the surrounding areas. You were expected to work a seven hour day, five days a week for which you were paid a wage each week. A canteen administered by Screws sold most things except alcohol, if it was legal you could buy it.

Unlock was at seven a.m. each workday morning, eight a.m. weekends, breakfast was available from a hot-plate if you wanted it. The food was about as good as it gets for a prison, there were few complaints from the gourmet sector, or from the gluttons. Cooking facilities were available on each wing for the affluent and more fastidious inmates who liked to dine on civilian food.

One-upmanship was a phenomenon practised by the gangster element who regularly preened themselves with thick gold crucifixes, Rolex watches the size of clocks, designer footwear, curtains and bedspreads ordered from Harrods. Ostentatious peacocks, they became known as the clown princes of crime. One of the comedians bought a Persian rug from Sotheby's for his cell. It cost the nut in excess of five thousand pounds. An embargo was placed on rings which were restricted to simple gold wedding bands otherwise the peacocks would doubtlessly be strutting the gantries adorned with diamonds the size of golf balls.

After the daily work shift the natives were marched back to the cell blocks and fed then banged up from five until six, after which the cells were unlocked for association which lasted until nine p.m. each night. A snooker and pool table was constantly on the go. A games room with darts and table soccer was an option as well as gym classes, badminton competitions, a television hall and educational classes were all on offer. Gambling was rampant with draw-poker and stud-poker schools playing at every opportunity. Home-made booze was always being brewed and bent Screws brought in vodka and other illicit goods. Weekend parties celebrating a birthday or an imminent release were not unusual; the Screws turned a blind-eye, content with ogling pornographic magazines and cracking comic book crosswords.

Several guys who sprang from the same shiftless streets of despair that produced me and quite a number of career outlaws welcomed me to the ranch. Henry F., who lived in the next road to me, was ten years into a life sentence for a particularly gruesome murder. Jimmy T., a body building buddy, was a mate of my brother; he was doing time for armed robbery and the irrepressible Delroy was serving a nine year stretch for a paper thin conspiracy. A spaghetti bolognaise meal was prepared accompanied by a bottle of vodka, a far cry from the tribulations experienced since my arrest. I relaxed, ate decent food and savoured a drink in the company of friends from the old neighbourhood.

Henry had regressed mentally since I last saw him some four years earlier. A lifer parole review board notified him that his case would not be considered for review until at least another ten years had elapsed. A burden too difficult for him to handle and so he sought a psychological crutch prescribed by the in-house medical staff. His bloodstream was an open inlet for mind-bending anti-psychotic tranquillisers inducing a vacuous expression, enhanced dilation of the pupils transforming his features to that of a natter-jack toad, his speech was slurred - the guy was cabbaged by constant drug overloading. I felt pity for this once strong character who had succumbed to penal pressure resulting in the abandonment of his spirit. A lost soul. Henry eventually lost the plot; paranoia bubbled away inside his demented skull. He flew into the wing governor's office carrying a playboy magazine and screaming abuse that an article was deliberately put in there by the governor to test his reaction. He locked the door and attacked the wing governor before Screws managed to rescue the bloodied and bruised bureaucrat. Henry was subdued, injected with restraining chemicals and was eventually smuggled from Hull to Ashworth, an asylum for the criminally insane. No gentle free-world breeze will ever touch the cheeks of the doomed Henry; the only time he will be paroled is when the cemetery gates open to cast a dark shadow over the hearse bearing his cardboard casket.

Drugs were never a factor during my last spell in the gulags, tobacco and cash being the source of most transactions between the inmates. In the three years or so since I was an involuntary guest, the usage of narcotics had proliferated to such a degree that cannabis had replaced both cash and tobacco as the means of currency. This was the advent of the serious drug dealer, the lost souls were puffing their brains away, addicted to the cannabis coma subculture, spending their jailhouse wages on the fog inducing guff. Jimmy the Jock, a knife fighting Glaswegian was the principal dealer on the cell block. He was a chest-beating bully who surrounded himself with feeble minded mules who carried chunks of pot stuffed inside their rectums. He assumed the mantle of a mafia don, bossing the shower of creeps to do his bidding and paying for their loyalty with small doses of dope.

The 'Don' waltzed about the tiers clad in shorts, boots and a Celtic football shirt, collecting debts from his addict clientele. He was in his early forties with grey closely cropped hair, a large Roman head, saucer shaped eyeballs which continually bobbed about in their sockets, dwarfish in stature but stockily built, he reminded me of a pit-pony. Forever boasting of vicious acts of violence that he had perpetrated during his criminal campaigns. According to his fables he had sliced and slashed more human carcasses than an abattoir butcher has skinned cattle. He had a rapacious nature which he used to exploit the more vulnerable residents, mainly lifers who had been abandoned by family and friends; most were in debt to the 'Don' and they paid their prison earnings over to him each week.

He didn't possess the status or the covert dexterity to inspire the trust to have a bent Screw on the payroll and so his supply of narcotics was smuggled in through the prison visiting block. Gossip around the poker table had it that one of his mules could fit a rugby ball inside his well-greased rectum; it was purported that this human depositary had regularly shoved half a kilo up his box on visiting days.

Horse gambling preoccupied a good percentage of the population, especially when televised. It was a lucrative business and moreover, it was sanctioned by the administration. A cockney bank robber serving eighteen years controlled the bookmaking business; he would take any bet and his reputation as a fair man was justified. I had plenty of time for him, a man of honour. Some of the gamblers lost small fortunes to him over the years. I know of one gangster who paid him two to three grand every month, dropping the cash off at his brother's house. He made life a lot easier for me by supplying all the necessary funds required to ease the anguish of coping with years of repressive abnormality.

A huge compound upon which inter-wing football matches were played most weekends and during the summer nights provided an opportunity for various nefarious plots to be debated and contraband deals to take place. A lot of feuds were settled out on the compound under the cover of clusters of convicts herded together like cattle in a pen. A cowardly thrust with a home-made blade into an unsuspecting victim's torso was a speciality of the knife fighting Jocks.

I had been on the wing roughly three days when a lifer approached me with a budgie on his shoulder, he asked if I wished to buy the talking bird cheaply. I recognised him as Tony C, who served time in Wakefield Prison when I was the bookmaker there. He was stark raving mad, a born loser who couldn't pick a winner in a two horse race. Tony was riddled with psychoses and could be found loitering around the cell-block toilets with a towel hung over his arm, he was a hygiene freak constantly scrubbing his hands. This six-foot-five beanpole, with a massive misshapen head, who resembled the infamous Elephant man, looked as if he had ascended from the depths of Hell. Prison inspectors regularly toured the prison to ensure the inmates' human rights were not being breached. Nutty Tony would dash after them carrying his battered tea stained case depositions, pestering the bureaucrats to read them, whilst screaming that he was an innocent man.

A prisoner was bludgeoned to death in his cell during my spell at another prison. A police investigation ensued culminating in every prisoner in the wing being interviewed by the Police. The jail was on a lock-down; four prisoners at a time where escorted to the interview room, three sat outside whilst one was being questioned; the conversational exchange could be overheard by the waiting trio. I was waiting my turn when Tony loped in, depositions in hand, totally oblivious to the recently murdered inmate.

"OK Tony, where was you between seven-thirty and eight-thirty yesterday morning?" a smart ass young detective asked politely, his colleague sitting alongside him taking notes.

"Never fuckin' mind, I wasn't here when this murder got done. Read these pal, I'm an innocent man," Tony yelled loudly at the officer as he tried to shove his case file in the detective's face.

"Tony, we're here investigating a prison murder, we don't have the time to read your file. Where were you yesterday morning?" the copper asked benignly to the increasingly agitated nutter.

"I shouldn't be here, I was fitted up by you dirty bastards. Now fuckin' read them," Tony roared, his latent lunacy steaming through his brain.

The two detectives realised they were getting nowhere fast with this madman and decided to terminate the interview. "OK Tony, just sign this at the bottom and you can go." The frustrated and somewhat mesmerised copper stated. "Fuck you," the loon screamed loudly. The sounds of a scuffle and chairs being banged could be heard. The office doors burst open and Tony dashed out followed closely by the cop. "He's swallowed my Parker pen! The nutcase has swallowed my Parker pen," the bemused and almost tearful cop shouted to the Screws who swiftly pounced on the choking Tony and restrained him before ferreting him off to the hospital.

I politely refused the semi-illiterate abomination's offer to buy a budgie; the idiot then asked if I would look through his case files and assist him in lodging a futile appeal. I had drafted numerous appeal applications in the past, mainly for wrongly convicted inmates who struggled with the English language. Tony was aware of this fact hence his opening gambit with the sale of a silly bird.

"Tony, I went through the transcripts before; the evidence against you is overwhelming and irrefutable. You are guilty mate, so do yourself and me a favour and fuck off," I emphatically asserted, dismissing this babbling bundle of mental disorders from my cell. He heeded my advice, trotting off to the nearest recess where he spent twenty minutes sulking while he scrubbed his well washed hands. All I needed was this nut pestering me; his grasp on reality was gossamer thin and just as tenuous.

I heard he was found many years later, hanging from his cell bars, dead and ultimately free from his living nightmares.

I sought temporary refuge in the solitude of my cell away from the gibberish spewing forth from the mouth of the self-proclaimed innocent man.

CHAPTER 13

Assimilating into Hull's society after two years of endless squabbling with National Front acolytes in the backwaters of the short-term correctional facilities proved to be a welcome relief. Apart from the oddballs, it was a piss easy way to sacrifice a chunk of one's allocated life-span. Occupational therapy was the game plan to retain mental acumen; a regular physical training routine based on plenty of cardio-vascular exercise to stem the ageing process and preserve self-confidence in anticipation of liberation day.

Months soon crept by - I had established a routine of morning gymnasium classes followed by daily tuition in the jail's educational block. The gunshot traumatised arm was responding well to a physiotherapy workout set by one of the instructors. Evenings were taken up gambling on the card tables; I played stud-poker most nights except Saturdays when we usually managed to have a good drink, either home-made beer or smuggled-in vodka.

A couple of guys from Liverpool arrived at this particular point in time with whom I was quite familiar. They were convicted of importing a ton of cannabis into Liverpool docks which came as a surprise to me as they were career thieves specialising in stealing lorry loads of swag. I had experienced a few bits of business with them in the past and regularly bumped into them in the clubs and drinking dens that flourished after hours in the shadowy back alleys of down-town Liverpool. I met up with one of the convicted narcotic importers on the compound. Joe, a thirty year old thief, recounted his tale of woe as we walked around the perimeter inhaling the fresh odourless air.

"How did you get into that fuckin' shit drug business?" I asked the professional thief.

"Fuckin' greed, mate. You know we always grafted the wagons and the docks, got a decent living, no hassle from the Old Bill. Anyway, one of the chaps has a cousin and the fuckin' cousin's got African seamen bringing bags of cannabis through the docks, he wants to start upping the ante by bringing a hundred kilos in at a time." Joe paused, shaking his head regrettably as his unfortunate choice surfaces to haunt him. "He approaches us with an offer of ten grand for every parcel we bring through. Happy fuckin' days. We have no problem sorting it, every six weeks or so, bingo, we pick up a parcel, deliver it and get paid the ten large," he explained tentatively as he continued to shake his head in a show of dissatisfaction at his plight.

"Good wages for fuck-all. How did you come unstuck?" I enquired, curious to discover the cause of his personal disaster.

"We start thinking... if we are paid ten grand for getting the gear off the fuckin' docks how much money are these guys making. We have a meet and ask for a piece of the action, they cut us in, no problem. We get a few parcels through and everybody is like Jack-the-fuckin'-lad, top of the range cars and jewellery, champagne flowing out of our fuckin' ears. Charlie wants to be big licks and looks to buy a club off your pal, Fat Sid. We've got plenty of spare readies so we meet up with Sid, start fuckin' partying with him and end up giving him a lump of cash for this place he owned in town." Joe continued his recital about his downfall a typical tirade of wanton need a trait that fills prisons and ministerial Cabinets.

"Don't tell me Joe, you bent Fat Sid in on the fuckin' graft," I interceded, believing that Fat Sid would seize any opportunity to hitch his fat ass-hole to a money making scheme. In retrospect Sid probably pawned the group of smugglers.

"Right he fuckin' did. We all end up grafting together. Sid has another way of smuggling the shit using containers into the docks; he sorted the paperwork so we can just drive the cannabis through the dock gates, also he had a bent cop for insurance. We had a dummy run with a couple of hundred kilos, it pissed in. We all thought this was fuckin' legal 'cos we weren't robbing anything, there's no screams in the papers. Next fuckin' thing we throw a ton on the container, we pull it off the dock and unload it in a slaughter. No fuckin' problem mate. A day later we're in the slaughter sorting the gear when the doors come crashing off the fuckin' hinges and an army of plod and Customs officers steam in and knock the fuck out of us." He concluded his account of his mishap, distraught because he was captured but with no remorse for the crime itself. I asked about Sid's involvement.

"Did Fat Chops get pulled in for questioning mate?" I enquired to allay curiosity bubbling in the corridors of my mind.

"No, he never got a tug. He was never hands-on, he just sorted the paperwork down to bogus fuckin' companies. He stayed well away and kept his hands squeaky clean. He's got no fuckin' bottle for graft. He took care of us though once we got lifted, Y'know, sorted briefs out, got us sureties for bail," he informed me, displaying an air of confidence in Sid's credentials as a solid upstanding villain.

Joe and his crew of smugglers were pioneers in the organisation of large scale importation of narcotics; they were amongst the first to be arrested and indicted from Liverpool. It was a novelty crime at the time, producing vast profits for little risk. A novelty that became a magnet attracting the attention of every criminal in the land. Tales about the gang of smugglers' exploits made them very popular crooks who were targeted by London gangsters, armed robbers, safe-crackers, hijackers, kidnappers, even sophisticated burglars - all wanted to verify the sums of money generated and the source of Joe's drugs. He was a celebrity convict who was as popular as Elvis at this moment in criminal history.

Retrospective analysis of Joe and the demise of his band of importers reveals the deceitful fingerprints of Fatso weaving the web that snared them. Over the decades, countless criminals were incarcerated after embracing schemes touted by this twisted tongued covert operative. He was a master of deception. Joe and his team of importers never suspected that they were mere pawns to be sacrificed at the whim of Fat Sid and his police handlers. I was unaware of the nature of this specimen's covert status when I conversed with Joe the importer. It took decades before the chameleon's true colour was exposed.

Delroy waltzed through the jail without a care in the world, nothing ever seemed to bother him, a smile and a funny quip was his stock in trade, he was chairman of the prison debating society and pestered me to participate in the Friday night sessions organised by Chaplain Hamish. Hamish was a tall foppish man with premature balding hair laced across his bulbous head, he was gangly and sloppily dressed and looked about forty. I was introduced to Hamish by the dictatorial Delroy who overpowered Hamish by the sheer force of his personality. The chaplain seemed at first glance to be of dubious gender, he was overtly camp, flitting about, his limp wrist flapping each time he approached Delroy. He was obviously enamoured by this articulate muscle man.

A core of regular middle aged females were the basis of the Friday night debates, guests from various universities and colleges were usually invited to bolster the outside team. Approximately a dozen outsiders turned up each week; Hamish laid on tea, coffee and biscuits. Two Screws were on hand but sat at the rear of the chapel keeping a check on the proceedings.

Each week a topic for conversation was posted and the two opposing teams would discuss the matter applying logic and a degree of common sense. Biblical connotations usually had some bearing on the chosen subject, something I viewed with a cynical and jaundiced eye. The prison team consisted mainly of loopy lifers who scrubbed their flesh with scented soap, brushed their tobacco stained teeth and dressed in their best prison-issue rags. They had joined the Friday night debate not for their verbal dexterity and the joy of exercising their tonsils but to fantasize over the regular female frumps. On the other hand, Delroy was a serious debater, a true thespian possessing excellent oratorical skills, forever playing a role. Hamish involved Delroy in all aspects of the prison chapel functions, particularly the Sunday-morning services. If it were possible the infatuated chaplain would have got the role-playing, piss-taking Delroy ordained as a priest; Delroy would have excelled in the part. He was a man of intellect who wandered down the road to perdition, a path he chose like most of the sinners in the slammer. He could have succeeded in whatever legitimate field he chose to follow, however the thrill of the criminal caper proved to be more alluring to this career criminal.

Ken a pony-tailed lifer was the waiter and tea maker of the debating society, a fifty-year-old tall well-built charmer. He had spent two decades inside for a catalogue of particularly heinous crimes and was fated to spend the rest of his days pottering about the jailhouses. Ken had adjusted to this factor and made the most of what little prison had to offer. Mingling with the female guests was the highlight of his existence. He fluttered around the dowdy maidens handing them tea and biscuits whilst complimenting them on their dress code, remarking on their beauty, the very epitome of grace and courtesy was displayed by Ken the kitchen sink killer.

Hamish clapped his manicured hands together indicating it

was time for the debate to begin. Both teams settled in their respective areas and prepared for verbal interplay. Delroy eventually graced the floor with a dramatic diatribe littered with classic quotations with the odd Biblical reference tossed in, he delivered his argument with the skill of a Shakespearian actor striding the boards of some great stage. I couldn't contain myself laughing loudly at his histrionics; he was amusing himself but Hamish and the other participants couldn't see it.

It wasn't long before the topic deteriorated to incorporate penal politics tactfully brought into the session by a section of institutional men who loved to air their gripes about prison affairs. First, it was the unfairness of the parole board, then someone complained that his trial was rigged and all the jury members were police officers; the poor quality of prison food was vilified described as offal, then some lifer argued that dogs should be allowed on visits. Delroy intervened several times stating they were digressing from the forum's topic, ordering them to return to the posted subject but to no avail. He stood there grinning at me highly entertained by this rag-tag bunch of misfits.

I departed from the evening determined never to go again. A kindergarten would have been a more appropriate setting for the crowing convicts. I much preferred the company of the poker players.

I continued to pursue a rigorous training regime in the gym. I was regaining the weight that fell off after the bullet wounds to my arm and chest. Delroy had the food situation sorted so that we had a steady supply of quality meat to supplement our penal diet. I presume Hamish supplied the meat and other ingredients that added to our nightly cooked meals. Jimmy the self-ascribed mafia don strutted the landings, his croaky voice grating on the nerves as he bawled out the names of his pot punters. Each night he habitually swaggered up and down the various landings getting orders for narcotics before dispatching his mules to deliver the drugs. His jaunts would sometimes be interrupted when he would enter a cell to intimidate a user whose drug debt was getting out of hand. He seldom approached our neck of the woods, we acknowledged him but had little time for him and his way of life.

A couple of bank robbers got parole which boosted the hopes of the optimists who believed that if they got it why not me. This dangling carrot was an effective tool in stemming violence and penal rebellion. Hard-core felons grasped the carrot of hope refraining from confrontational situations with Screws and to a lesser degree their fellow prisoners. A game was enacted, some of these robbers adopted the persona of choir boys attending church on a Sunday morning; some even joined up for Hamish's Bible-reading classes.

Sunday mornings would see the parole hunters dashing to the prison chapel, jostling each other out of the way as they fought to sit on the front pew by the altar and adjacent to the governor's pew. These hypocrites had perpetrated vicious robberies for profit and now pretended to have found God in the faint hope of gaining premature release. Hard-core creeps became the title bestowed upon the front pew squatters who were the brunt of Delroy's weekly readings from the pulpit. He ad-libbed his sermons to assail the prostitution of their morality as they perched on the front pews like law-abiding citizens.

Months drifted by and the pattern of life replicated - a weekly booze up served to break the monotony and relieve jailhouse stress. The poker school is in full swing, I'm sitting in, enjoying a run of luck when the loud unmistakable voice of Jimmy the knife fighting Jock booms across the landings. Threats of mayhem and intents to disembowel the culprit sprayed from the lips of the loud-mouth bully.

"I fuckin' warn the lot of you bastards. Get my fuckin' money back or I'll cut you to fuckin' pieces. Slag bastards," he screamed at all the guys playing cards, then sped off before anyone could reply. His aggressive attitude displeased a number of serious people. He darted about the wing screaming abuse, gesturing with his hands the damage he intended to inflict with his tool to the thief who had the temerity to steal his stash.

Apparently he had a stash of money earned from his drug enterprise secreted on the wing and someone had stolen it which enraged the chest-beating idiot. He was rampaging around the wing bellowing loudly like a fatally wounded animal, his hysteria obviously attracting the attention of the authorities with inevitable repercussions.

The following day the prison was on a lock-down, a posse of Screws descended on the wing ransacking the cells searching for contraband and the mouthy Jock's weapons. Nobody was fed until the early evening with the Jock being cursed by several entombed inmates. He reacted with a fusillade of expletives hurled through his window at all and sundry, denouncing their mothers as whores, then challenging all comers to a knife fight. A challenge that in the course of time would no doubt be accepted.

Two days of lock-down, the search completed to the satisfaction of the security officers, a few weapons were discovered, several batches of home-made booze were found then poured down the drains much to the annoyance and rage of the brewers. No sums of money were uncovered, neither were any narcotics found; the Screws were reluctant to poke and pry up the rectums of suspected mules. Normality resumed with all the natives back in the groove and a host of convicts clearly aggrieved by the asinine behaviour of the knife-man which lost them their home-made alcohol. A few words were exchanged between aggrieved factions but the Jock seemed unperturbed

- making a lot of noise when confronted. His noise-making tactics fooled nobody - it was a ploy to protect himself from an imminent attack. He became subdued, the swagger gone from his step, his mules still huddled close to him but most of the wing gave him the cold shoulder.

A couple of weeks had elapsed since the lock-down caused by the mega mouthed Jock. One of his human depositories had come through with a big chunk of dope and he appeared to be back in business. Lifers were puffing away like funnels on a steamship. He gained back a bit of self-belief and let his guard down. It was breakfast time; I had just filled a flask with boiling water and I was returning to my cell for a coffee when I noticed a rumpus around the office. A posse of officers in a state of alarm, shuttling inmates to their cells, doors being slammed, voices shouting loudly.

I paused, scanning the scene to see if I could detect anything amiss.

A Screw ascended onto the landing banging everyone up, he approached my cell.

"Behind your door Scouse," he orders curtly, a worried look etched upon his face.

"Somebody had it away mate?" I asked the Screw curious to the security alert.

"No, somebody has attacked the Jock," he retorted as he swiftly banged me up. I relaxed, made myself a coffee and then waited for the details of the attack on the Don to filter along the grapevine as the caged prisoners shouted out of the cell windows. A voice I identified as Delroy beckoned me to my cell window and I clambered up in response.

"Somebody plunged the Jock. He's been rushed to hospital Tom. He's still breathing so I guess he must have said his prayers last night." A long loud burst of laughter erupted from Delroy as he imparted news regarding the savage attack on the mafia impersonator. I climbed down from the cell window and flopped on my bunk; a stabbing if fatal usually resulted in a day or so lock-down.

The stabbed victim never returned to the prison; he suffered an horrendous injury which paralysed him leaving him a paraplegic unable to walk. An assailant had crept into his cell at unlock while the Don was dozing in his bed and then brutally rammed a long metal spike into his stomach which exited through his back. Such was the force of this calculated attack that the spike pinned the hitherto man of violence to the mattress. He was subsequently moved to hospital with the mattress still attached to his bloody torso. Rumour had it that he was transferred to a unit in Scotland where he was given a wheel chair to roam about the grounds in, feeding the birds and informing passers-by of his prowess as a great warrior before being struck down by an assassin.

Nobody was ever charged with the attempted murder of the narcotic dealing bully; two inmates were mentioned in dispatches as the likely suspects, they were ghosted out for an extended tour of the isolation units in the bowels of the numerous assessment facilities scattered across the English landscape.

His moronic mules dispersed his cache of drugs around the wing to all the smokers in an effort to curry favour with a disgruntled clientele. They lived in fear of retribution after their protector and mentor had been taken down; eventually they scuttled away into the shadows and social obscurity.

CHAPTER 14

Like Hydra, the void left by the demise of the drug supplying Jock was instantly replaced by Hector a Mancunian with roots in the black community. Demand exceeded supply making for a lucrative business which the fair minded Hector duly set up and flourished.

I was into my third year, cruising along, when a guy visited from the home front to inform me that Vinnie was seen in Liverpool. I dismissed this as idle gossip but the guy who was a connected villain insisted the snippet of data was factual. I knew that Vinnie was incarcerated in Long Lartin, a prison in the Midlands, so I persuaded Delroy to use his influence with Hamish to find out the authenticity of the gossip. A couple of days later he verified that Vinnie had been granted parole and was on a pre-release home leave. This was a miracle of Biblical proportions equivalent to walking on water or raising the dead. It was incomprehensible that a career thief would be paroled first, and moreover for an act involving firearms. He in fact performed a feat comparable to swimming the English Channel underwater whilst holding his breath. The Holy Grail fell into his palms opening sealed gates allowing him to walk free after spending a little over three years inside the jailhouses. I served more than double this, eight years in fact for exactly the same crime, this baffled me for many a day.

Circumstantial analysis of the parole enigma pointed to the putrid influence of Fatso; he probably redeemed himself by utilising his contacts in the law enforcement agencies to pull rank and rubber stamp Vinnie's parole. A seed of hope momentarily planted itself in my mind causing me to think that I might have a modicum of a chance of premature resurrection but it soon perished on the thorns of reality when I remembered that I was a category 'A' prisoner, which barred me from even applying for parole. Vinnie was indeed a lucky man being gifted a passport to freedom.

I forwarded the news of Vinnie's miracle to the front pew faithful who took heart and began to pray even harder for immediate salvation. Sunday morning they spruced themselves up to perfection as if they were to be inspected at a military passing out parade. It was raining this particular Sunday morning causing the cancellation of outdoor activities. I opted to watch Delroy's amateur theatrics at the chapel of hope and enjoy a few minutes of hilarity from the master piss-taker. Delroy was hovering about the altar, a Bible in his hand chattering away to Hamish. He was immaculately attired, starched shirt, tailored trousers, a pair of expensive brogues, a gold watch on his wrist; he waved as he noticed me sitting down, a broad grin lit up his features.

The chapel was located at the rear of the prison, it had seating capacity for a hundred and fifty souls but I doubted if that many ever attended. On one side sat the civilian church goers, governors, Screws, wives of the prison employees; on the other sat the convicts, murderers, thieves, bank robbers, rapists and the odd arsonist or two. Hamish appeared in the pulpit following an age old ritual of mumbo-jumbo about saints and saviours, a few examples of faith then a token hymn. He announced a reading by Delroy who needed no prompting as he leapt into the pulpit to preach to the philistines congregated before him.

He held the Bible in his extended right hand gazing about the chapel, his eyes coming to rest on the front pew gangsters;

he shook his head as a sign of admonishment then proceeded to read a passage from the Bible. There was a dramatic pause as he cast his eyes heavenwards; he pointed his index finger at the charlatans then rattled off a tirade.

"Sinners, you come into the house of the Good Lord himself, hiding behind a mask of piety and bogus intent; you worship and praise our Lord Jesus while your black sin-stained souls cavort with the devil. Salvation comes to those who truly repent not to those who masquerade as believers for their own selfish needs. Damnation… eternal damnation the burning fires of Hell will be your reward for living a lie in the house of our Good Lord." He delivered this condemnation of the charlatans with vigour and the occasional dramatic pause. I laughed all the way through his performance; he was amusing himself by ridiculing the game-playing parole seekers, who hung their heads shamelessly as they sat and absorbed a tirade aimed at them and their blatant hypocrisy.

On the wing, after the charade in the chapel, Delroy was buzzing over his oratorical piece from the pulpit. He found it difficult to contain his laughter when he wagged his finger at the front-pew frauds.

"Did you see the look on their faces when I criticised their hypocrisy? I was about to start giggling. I thought about Laurence Olivier's Othello to help me stop the giggles. He burst out laughing at his theatrical performance which fooled the faithful congregation. He then tells me that he tried to persuade Hamish to let him wear one of his cassocks next time he delivers a sermon. The chaplain of course refused him.

A political proclamation by the incumbent Home Secretary shattered the hopes and dreams of the church going crew; parole would be unavailable to all inmates serving four years and over convicted of a violent crime. This vote catching declaration included nearly all the prisoners incarcerated in the long term institutions where the minimum tariff was five years. A typical vote catching ruse drummed up by the Faustian female, Old Iron Pants, Thatcher, the most reviled person in the gulag system. This power-mad maiden with the false voice, surrounded herself with sycophantic men who acquiesced to her every amoral whim, Leon Brittan was no exception when he made his retroactive proclamation.

This impacted upon the lives of many long-term robbers who struggled to maintain a family relationship with wives and children. Leon increased the burden by turning out the light in their fantasy-land tunnels.

Within the jail, attitudes underwent a metamorphism from compliance to disobedience, the carrot of control removed from the jailhouse by a silly puppet in the interest of political capital. Common sense would have dictated that you bring in the embargo by stealth instead of jumping into television studios and broadcasting the fact globally. It certainly affected the front-pew mob who, on hearing that the parole board had been disbanded and they were no longer eligible for parole, boycotted the prison chapel, started plotting anarchy and began brewing beer with all the rest of the guys.

Most of the staff were disgusted by the Home Secretary's stupidity prohibiting parole for violent acts causing mutiny and animosity inside the gulags. The Screws on the front line were fuming as they daily faced the wrath of penal discontent. The antidote to appease the disgruntled Screws and bolster their flagging moral was to award them a pay rise which was a successful tactic of the money-mad Thatcher Junta. It worked to subjugate the Valiant Miners during their epic strike whereupon The Junta bribed the police to brutalise the struggling miners into submission; it certainly pacified the hitherto restless Screws into total compliance. I believe their salaries almost doubled, money had transformed them into acolytes of government policy.

I was on a family visit one day when the brazen bun-faced Leon Brittan waltzed in with an entourage of suited aides led by the main prison governor. Approximately twenty inmates plus their visitors were camped at the tables when this bundle of flabbiness coasted in, a fraudulent smile etched upon his spotty face. He stood by the tea counter extending his verbosity to a couple of W.V.S. helpers who blushed with pride as if royalty had spoken to them. Most of the convicts on the visit recognised this fat quirky head of the jail system, who had added years to their sentences with his jiggery-pokery; his presence engendered rumblings of dissatisfaction amongst the tables. The bumbling buffoon moved about the room, bodyguard in tow, trying to engage people in conversation but was more or less blanked, a cockney visitor whose husband was serving eighteen years began to scream at him.

"You dirty Tory bastard. My Husband's doing an extra five years down to you. Cunt!" she shrieked loudly like a banshee startling the fancy dressed party of politicians. Silly bollocks turned crimson looking at the governor to bail him out of an embarrassing situation.

Her outburst was like a battle cry arousing the adrenalin of a few other despondent natives who joined in the argument berating the minister, who wished the ground would open up and swallow him. A passionate and extremely animated bunch of miscreants chanted abuse showering the embattled Billy Bunter double with expletives, denouncing his parents and questioning his gender. He was quickly led out of the hostile visiting room bemused and bedraggled by the deep abhorrence displayed towards him. Any idiot would have avoided this kind of confrontation but such was the arrogance of the man and his politics that he assumed he would be greeted by a chorus of cheering hosannas.

A prominent member of the parole hunters accosted me after the visit to ascertain if that cheeky bastard Brittan had slumped about in the visiting area. I told him that he had put in an appearance. He flew into a rage;

"I'd have shot that bastard in the head," he screamed.

I nodded and got off. I don't know where he was going to get the gun from, maybe from the God he prayed to every week when he thought he had a chance in the parole lottery stakes.

Secularisation seeped into the mind-set of the faithful, Hamish and the pulpit posing Delroy were pontificating to an empty chapel, the front pew being occupied by a pair of religious lifers who had lost everything including their minds; the Bible-reading class was also greatly depleted. Delroy had lost his enthusiasm to perform; there was no challenge for him to take the piss out of a couple of retards. He instructed Hamish to drum up more spectators otherwise he too would abandon the faith.

During this period, over a game of chess, Delroy asked me to consider joining forces with him when we are free to start up a religion. He attempted to convince me that it was far more lucrative than crime, it was in essence the greatest money making scam in the history of mankind. We parody Christianity; instead of a crucifix as a symbol we invent our own, a holy fish or something. Christianity is based on two concepts, the Immaculate Conception and the Resurrection; refute those two concepts and the whole basis of the creed dissolves into the heavens from where it allegedly descended.

"A whole world of gullible fools are waiting out there Tom. Look at those raconteurs from the Bible belt in America, they own private jets, live in mansions, fornicating with beautiful woman all earned from the pockets of idiots who believe all the bullshit spouted by these confidence tricksters. I'll be the Messiah - a prophet to make a profit and to bamboozle the weak minded susceptible faith seekers with my rhetorical talent. It is not beyond our scope to get into this religious business. He droned on describing a new evolutionary religion based on Darwinism.

He was positive that there was a fortune to be had from the feeble minded masses who for generations had made the established religions into multi-national global corporations worth billions and who manufactured nothing except faith. His brief spell assisting the foppish Hamish had planted the seeds of exploitation in his scheming brain. I declined his offer but appreciated his analysis.

Escape plans were forever being discussed, more so since the abolishment of parole; the desperado factions would base their plots on violence such as hostage-taking, then demanding transport from the authorities otherwise they would dispose of the hostages. Anyone with half a brain would discount these proposals as ludicrous but one or two were attempted over the years with predictably disastrous results. A couple of Irish freedom fighters serving monumental life sentences, with whom I shared a Saturday night drink, were constantly plotting to escape and they had explored every feasible avenue; they concluded it was almost impossible. A view shared by most but it still didn't deter inmates from contemplating the prospect. In the midst of a boozing session a suggestion was made about an escape being made from the compound during association when a football match was being played. It was rubbished as impracticable at first but as time passed it gained in momentum. We analysed the possibilities.

Dicky arrived at the jailhouse after an odyssey that included a brief stay at most of the gulag's dirtiest, smelly urinals; he had endured this ordeal since the fracas during the sewing circle class at Wormwood Scrubs. This tactic was a customary inconvenience applied to Republicans by a spiteful penal authority who did not hide their contempt for the Irish rebels. He had weathered the hardship well, emerging with his wit and mind as sharp as ever. I began to draft proclamations for him that he sent out to be published in the Republican News. I regularly compiled these declarations which gave me an insight into the Cause for which they fought so determinedly. Stripped bare of the prejudiced English propaganda their grievance was justifiable and understandable. A resolution could never be achieved with elected Prime Ministers having the intransigence and colonial jack-boot mentality of Thatcher. If she had her way, she would bomb the resistance out of the freedom fighting rebels.

Dicky was soon incorporated into the plot to escape because of his experience in the helicopter hijacking that cost him his freedom. Quite a few would-be plotters attempted to pick his brains regarding the idiosyncrasies of helicopter flight before and after the event.

I drafted a petition to the Home Office explaining the implications that abolishment of parole had on long-term prisoners; I criticised the morality of it, especially that its enforcement was retroactive, a factor that didn't take into account the original sentence imposed by a judge who must have considered the defendants chance of parole when passing sentence. This petition was signed by most of the jailhouse and received the customary negative response from a Home Office errand boy.

A protest was planned against Billy Bunter Brittan's abolishment of parole. Instead of retreating to their cells after evening association, it was agreed that a sit-in would be staged in the television room. All hands slowly drifted into the television room, some of the guys stocking up with flasks of tea, others carting in a blanket or two. The onlooking Screws guessed something abnormal was afoot but lacked the initiative to intercede. A bell rang signalling the end of association and for all inmates to bang up for the night. Instead, there was a mass migration to the T.V. room. A posse of Screws were bewildered as their shouts of 'All away' were ignored. They huddled about, frustrated and confused awaiting the arrival of leadership for instructions as their mutton minds struggled to cope. Roughly eighty men participated in the demonstration, a show of unified disgust at an unjust political act against defenceless soft targets with no means of challenging the impropriety of Bunter's vote catching opportunism.

Reinforcements arrived attempting to coerce the protesters to abandon their futile cause and return to their respective cells, this was rejected by the more aggressive elements who threatened carnage if the Screws wanted a confrontation. They decided to negotiate, an assistant governor who had recently graduated from a university with a degree in sociology, asked for a delegation of prisoners to come to the door of the television room and explain the grievances. Lenny a bank robber put himself forward as a spokesman for the rebellious inmates, Booth a nutty lifer insisted on going with him. Lenny articulated the deep sense of injustice that the Home Secretary had implemented, a provocative ruling that would add years to most of the prisoners' jail terms. We believe that his ruling should only affect prisoners convicted after the announcement, not those already serving a prison term. The graduate agreed but stated he was powerless to do anything about it. However he would forward an account of the grievance to the Home Office immediately.

Booth, an extremely aggressive killer, was having none of

the graduate's placatory guff. Booth was a large, wild-looking man in his mid-forties and going nowhere, a penal lost soul, eyeballs protruding from the sockets like a pair of cricket balls, he assailed the young assistant governor and screamed as he grabbed the poor effeminate assistant in a vice like grip.

"Fuck you! Get that prick up here or you're gonna get an early fuckin' funeral."

This unpredictable lifer's behaviour alerted the attention of most of the protesters, he could escalate a peaceful demonstration into a blood bath. A couple of the more sensible guys remonstrated with the nut telling him to release his hold on the trembling and petrified A.G. The wild man reluctantly released the rubbery legged graduate who fled faster than an Olympic sprinter to hide behind a wall of Screws. Booth screamed sexual abuse after him.

These loose cannons were a danger to us all; an act of gross violence by Booth or another nut would reflect badly on every man in the room. The authorities would find each prisoner equally culpable which would certainly increase the prison sentences considerably.

A careful eye was kept on Booth and his fellow lunatics.

The A.G. had a breakdown and was duly whisked off to convalescence; a wise old senior officer stepped into the breach and used a softly-softly approach, openly condemning Thatcher's marionette Bunter's repressive reforms as barbaric. He promised that all the officers would back a recommendation for the incumbent Home Secretary to remove the retroactive clause from the parole reform schedule. Several officers reinforced this proposal and to further appease the protesters the senior officer offered everyone chips and ham suppers if they would abandon the protest and return to their cells peacefully. A vote was taking amongst the guys with just over half agreeing to capitulate by accepting the terms proffered. Booth, on whom the reason for the demonstration had no impact whatsoever with regard to his status as a life-term prisoner began calling everyone cowards and urging them to barricade themselves with him in the T.V. room. He had no takers as people drifted back to their cosy cells with bags of chips and ham clasped in their hands.

By unlock the next day, Booth and Lenny the bank robber had been ghosted out of the jail, no doubt put on the gulag merry-go-round, spending a year in the many segregation units peppered about the country.

CHAPTER 15

A ghost from the past returned to resurrect a nightmare experience I endured in the notorious House of Horrors - H.M.P. Wakefield. I had spent five years in this satanic cesspit of human misery for firearm offences; I had tasted the sweet fruits of freedom for only one year when I was ensnared in the Worcester catastrophe. I had smuggled numerous letters out of Wakefield Prison, letters that were countersigned by fifty other prisoners, exposing some of the institutionalised malpractices that were performed on the lost souls that inhabited the hidden dungeons within this mansion of madness. A rogue medical unit was functioning inside the jail's secret walls. Some of the smuggled mail was delivered to the Guardian newspaper and some to Michael Foot, a good socialist member of parliament. The letters aroused the interest of sectors of the press who asked the penal authorities to attest to the veracity of the allegations. Many left-wing politicians began to pressurise the authorities into having a public inquiry, pressure that ultimately transformed a barbaric system and toppled an abusive omnipotent regime.

One day, the governor summoned me to his hallowed halls, an event that was a precursor to bad news for the inmate. I viewed the invite with apprehension wondering what skeleton had leapt out of the past into the open that could further disrupt my capacity to cope. Much to my relief it was the smuggled letters and my part in the exposure of the medical misfits that ran the hospital facilities at Wakefield prison.

I was marched into the governor's office, a Screw standing either side of me, parodying a military tribunal with salutes and loud barking whilst stamping their leather boots on the wooden oak-stained floor.

A thick file was open on the desk in front of the governor who ignored me as he pretended to scrutinised my prison dossier. He shifted his eyes from the dossier to aim a cursory glance in my direction; he then coughed, cleared his throat, and then deigned to address me.

"Smith, you continue to pry and poke that nose of yours into matters that are no concern of yours. At Wakefield, you transgressed prison rules by communicating letters containing distorted accounts of prison affairs, via illegal channels, to proscribed media establishments." He paused and gave me a withering disdainful glare. I looked into his eyes, a smirk lighting up my face and I remained silent.

"These transgressions were on a previous sentence therefore I am powerless to punish you. However, it has come to my notice that you have been abusing the trust graciously bestowed upon you by the staff which permitted you access to a typewriter whilst doing course work in the education block. You have been responsible for drafting numerous appeals and petitions to the Home Office for other inmates; this is a clear breach of the privilege given to you. This privilege ceases forthwith as does your access to the educational facilities."

He droned on in a dull monotone as if he were talking to himself. He closed the dossier indicating the summons was over. I was offered an opportunity to defend myself but I knew it would be pointless, the angel Gabriel and the twelve disciples could not change a decision passed down by the number-one governor.

"Don't you think you should be thanking me for exposing the Nazi war criminals that were hiding out at that pisshole, Governor?" I blurted out sarcastically at his bowed head. Without looking up, he shouted to the Screws to escort me back to my cell.

Back in my cell, I lay down on my bunk, my mind drifting to the turbulent times spent inhaling oxygen in Wakefield's' chamber of horrors. Over four-hundred killers reside inside the chamber's caves - it was the main assessment centre in the U.K. determining whether the miscreants are criminally insane or just plain loopy. Wakefield had a self-contained hospital wing, fully equipped with operating theatre, proficient technicians and medical staff all under the supervision of Doctor Mengle a bow-tie wearing, six-foot-six beanpole of a man; he strolled about the prison sending shivers down the spine of lifers who crossed his vindictive path. This man controlled the psychiatry unit which had the power to deem whether a lifer is fit for release on licence or is incorrigible and should therefore never be released. Furthermore, the unit regularly classified inmates as criminally insane, earning the unfortunate sinner a one way ticket to Broadmoor, an asylum for the insane. Life-term natives feared Doctor Mengle more than Lucifer himself. He seemed to derive pleasure from his terrifying image, a permanent smile etched across his peanut shaped face, his eyes displaying an evil glint as they devoured the hopes of many of the jail's lifers with an icy stare condemning the recipient to eternal entombment.

On the wing where I resided, there were approximately eighty inhabitants serving life for murder; the other forty or so were a mixed bag of miscreants, robbers, pyromaniacs, a couple of Republicans, rapists and one or two paedophiles. Old Joe Conlon was on the wing, a truly innocent man fitted up by the immoral secret service steroid-heads for complicity in the Guildford bombing. I befriended Joe who used to dine with us each night, he suffered from a bad chest infection and should have been released on compassionate grounds. Everyone in the system was aware that he was an innocent man, as was his son Gerry but not one bureaucrat would reveal a gossamer thread of pity or mercy for fear of retribution from the governmental enforcement machinery. Compassion is a weakness - brutal vengeful penalty is strength. This appeared to be the motto of the incumbent administration. A man like Joe who had never committed a crime in his life, a simple man with simple values, buried alive because he lived in the wrong area of Belfast. He did not deserve the hand that fate dealt him. If the same circumstances arose that led to his incarceration but he had originated from the Shankhill area, he would not have been indicted. Geographical and sectarian roots convicted poor Joe, excluding him from the process of impartial justice. He deserved so much more than to die inside a prison, a victim of an overzealous prosecution and a dispassionate morally blind judiciary.

Years after Joe died he was exonerated along with all the other defendants in the case. A labour Prime Minister apologised to these victims of a grave miscarriage of justice, yet those guilty of perjury and abuse of the Law were never made accountable for their actions. They should have been shot at dawn or coerced to explain the reasons why they railroaded a patently innocent man.

Jonny Mac, a convicted killer had spent the past ten years on the cell block. He was regularly spotted jogging about the place, shadow boxing and tossing left hooks at the jaws of imaginary opponents. He had written to Angelo Dundee, a top American boxing manager, stating that he could beat any fighter in the world in his weight class and would he like to manage him once he was released. He certainly could throw a punch having knocked out several inmates who crossed his path. Jonny had no family or friends on the outside of prison, he hadn't received a visit for over five years. He was rudderless and destined to perish within the system because of his overt aggression.

He confided in me that he had been at the assessment

board who suggested to him that unless he volunteers for a lobotomy to eradicate the violent cells in his brain he will never be released. I thought he was joking at first but to my astonishment his tale was true. I advised him it was blackmail and to reject the proposal. I explained to the semi-literate inmate that having these cranks drilling holes in your skull is tantamount to suicide. My advice was ignored; Jonny opted for the gamble and shortly afterwards, Jonny the boxer disappeared off the wing.

Another lost soul was Bowser A. who looked after the wing snooker table located outside his cell. Bowser had spent over a decade behind bars for a couple of particularly gruesome murders using a claw hammer to batter his victims to death. Bowser was a heavily built, middle-aged Geordie. He had a notoriously short fuse - a walking time bomb who continually professed to be 'steaming', which suggested he was on the brink of a violent outburst. Bowser loved to bet on the horses. As the wing bookmaker, I regularly took his bets and over the years got to understand and pacify his bouts of madness. If a particular jockey got beaten causing his wager to lose he would go ballistic, threatening to inflict terrible damage on the jockey and the horse if only he could lay his hands upon them. His frustrated outbursts would reverberate around the cell block hitting the ears of the note-taking Screws, further damaging Bowsers minute chance of freedom.

I would lecture him about his verbal belligerence explaining that he was putting nails in his own coffin by showing his anger. Each time a Screw heard him threatening to kill someone, it would be logged and placed in his dossier. Play the game, start painting butterflies and flowers in your cell it's therapeutic; the shrinks love it; you will paint your way to freedom I explained to the bubbling neurotic killer.

A few weeks later Bowser approached me.

"Scouse I've took your advice, I got all the oil painting gear. Come an' see what I've painted man, it's a fuckin' masterpiece," he declared eagerly as he gripped my arm pulling me towards his cell, brimming with puerile excitement. I entered his cell where he pointed to a canvas upon which was painted a house with fire and smoke engulfing the building. Fearful faces could be seen looking out of the windows unable to escape the fire, the detail was quite good but the subject matter totally psychotic. I shook my head at the lunacy on display.

"Fuckin' brilliant! What do ya' think man?" The barmy Geordie exclaimed eager for my praise.

"You certainly can paint mate but why a fuckin' house on fire, why not trees, flowers or butterflies," I asked inquisitively whilst giving him a modicum of praise.

"The fuckin' shrink told me to paint the first thing that comes into my head. A fuckin' fire with all the bastards I hate burning inside was the first thing in my fuckin' head." Bowser's simplicity belied the madness that his explanation revealed.

"Listen, you let the bastards see that painting and tell them why you painted it and you will be in here for another ten stretch. Paint fuckin' flowers," I said to the barmpot, hoping to guide him away from his road to self-destruction.

"Fuck 'em, fuck the bastards, I'm not painting puffy flowers or faggotty fuckin' trees," his frustration and anger mounting, I nodded in agreement and retreated from this seething cauldron.

A few weeks after the exhibition of the blazing house, Bowser comes to my cell to collect some winnings from me, an occasion that raised his spirits for a while.

"Scouse I'm going to let the bastards sort my head out. I've signed up for the old brain treatment. They reckon if it works I'll be cured and be home before you can say Jack fuckin' shit," he announced full of excitement as if he'd just won the pools instead of jeopardising what bit of sanity remained at the hands of the Frankenstein cult lurking in the jail's sanatorium. I jumped off my bed in disbelief, I know the consequences of drilling holes in the skull, especially by this band of gung-ho apathetic jailhouse quacks.

"Don't go ahead with that bollocks mate - the pricks will cabbage you. Listen to me, its fuckin' deadly. Mengles is a stark raving nut." I attempted to persuade him from stepping into the unknown. I'd known Bowser for a few years and in spite of his hate-'em-all attitude, I liked him and wished him no harm.

"I've fuck-all to lose Scouse, I'm not gonna get out of here otherwise. Anyway if they fuck it up I'll strangle one of the bastards," he replied philosophically, his decision to accept this devil of a deal already sealed, his fate in the experimental palms of Quacks.

I spoke several times to Bowser about this situation attempting to persuade him to change his obdurate mind but to no avail. Bowser fell into the same category as Jonny the boxer, abandoned by society, no family or friends, no contact with the free world, nobody to complain if he vanished from the planet. Bowser was a prime candidate for the Frankenstein cult. One day I passed his cell, it was locked, his name card was gone and so was Bowser

The general consensus was that Bowser had moved to the silent secret world of the sanatorium, a sector of the institution that was isolated from the main population like some parallel universe controlled by paranoid aliens. In the five years I was confined in this madhouse I never once ventured into the hospital wing; any ailments were treated by a couple of male nurses who ran a small unit just off the prison centre where they dished out tranquilisers like sweets to all and sundry. One of the nurses looked like George Formby but instead of a ukulele he had an implement for syringing inmate's ears. He had a renowned fetish for pumping a soapy liquid into prisoner's ears whenever the opportunity presented itself. He was a typical maladjusted penal employee.

The third person that drifted off the wing in the direction of the drill and bit brigands was an arsonist named George. He had been sentenced to life for burning half the barns, haystacks and rural outbuildings across Yorkshire. He was a classic pyromaniac who exhibited all the symptoms associated with the malaise, a serial fire-bug who derived sexual pleasure from the fire and the ringing bells of the fire engines. I spoke to him asking why he rampaged through the farmlands burning property for the fun of it.

"It's bloody great, best thing ever Scouse, bloody flames shooting into the dark skies, firemen dashing about with bloody hoses, bells ringing, bloody marvellous."

His elation was obvious as he relived his escapades. George was mentally ill, he should have been a patient in an asylum receiving medication for his psychosis. I read through his depositions after he informed me that he had been in Wakefield for more than seventeen years. His mother had died ten years ago, he hadn't had a visit or a letter from outside since. His deposition revealed the depths of George's pyromania, he admits to masturbating at the scenes of the fires, a confession that earned him his life sentence and would probably prevent him from ever being released.

A few months elapsed, it was a warm summer's day and I was enjoying the fresh air, strolling around the perimeter of the compound debating the affairs of the cosmos with some sensible inmates when I had to side-step to avoid an inmate shuffling along slowly, his head bowed, muttering away to himself. I thought it was one of the numerous forgotten souls waiting for death to ease their misery, when I recognised the facial features of Jonny the boxer. I was so startled at the deterioration in his whole physical demeanour that I had to take a second look to make sure it was him - such was the decline in his appearance. He used to be a well-muscled very fit athlete with a full head of well-groomed hair who bounced about radiating health and vitality. Now he had physically shrunk, his head was mostly bald with clumps of hair protruding like garden weeds; his face had aged considerably and looked abnormally thin. My heart bled. I gripped his shoulder and shouted his name. He shrugged off my arm, looked at me but seemed not to identify me. He then turned and started to shuffle off. I caught up with him and tried to engage him in a conversation but my efforts were futile. The lights had gone out in Jonny's motionless eyes; the butchers had transformed him into a Zombie. I saw him twice more on the compound after this with the same negative results. Then he disappeared presumably to rot in the concealed shadows of the sanatorium.

A lot of the prisoners became wound up over the transformation imposed upon Jonny and made complaints to their respective wing assistant governors who were about as effective as inviting a deaf mute to a concert then asking what do you think of the music. The mute would probably be more beneficial to the cause than a platoon of assistant governors. Some of the guys wanted to take more drastic action but in a prison comprising mostly lifers who had killed their spouses, girlfriends, mothers or fathers, who in fact were not criminals but one-off offenders, it proved difficult to orchestrate a unified front to tackle the problem of brain amputation. A number of prisoners were ghosted out during the night for making threats towards the medical staff and daring to question the integrity of Mengles and his drill-bit cult.

The restlessness amongst the natives quickly subsided. Jonny the shadow boxer forgotten, normal routine resumed, apathy prevailed. I smuggled the first letter out to the press detailing the cabbaging of the boxer, his sentence and date of birth. It never got any publicity so the jailhouse cynics presumed it was shredded or treated as propaganda. Bowser emerged from the twilight medical coven a physical and mental wreck, a gibbering idiot, slobbering at the mouth, his robust belligerence cured but at an irredeemable price, the destruction of his personality in conjunction with a badly retarded brain. One of the staff intimated that this was normal procedure after such a major operation and in a couple of years old Bowser would be right as rain. I retorted that that was what the Nazis said when they experimented with the Jews in the Death Camps.

There were roughly fifty dependable guys in the entire jail, the rest were domestic killers or had committed crimes motivated by sexual abnormalities of one kind or another. A demonstration was organised on the compound in protest at the cabbaging process of prisoners by the asylum quacks. Fifty prisoners staged a sit-down in the yard refusing to return to the cells; the vast majority speedily dashed back for their tea. After a few hours a deputy governor addressed the protesters with a promise to look into the concerns raised and issue a statement in a day or so. The deluded and beguiled yard squatters swallowed the verbal excrement ending the sit-in and returned to the prison for a tray of chips and fish.

Ten of the protesters were shipped to other prisons the next morning; the rest were placed on disciplinary charges, I received a month in segregation.

More mail was drafted out to the press. I smuggled another letter to several M.P.s co-signed by fifty inmates who eventually created a ripple of response. Articles appeared in the press expressing concern about the cavalier approach by the Frankenstein cult in the way they lobotomised lifers with little or no consideration for the after effects of this pioneering surgery. Prisoners were treated like human guinea pigs by a cult of unbridled medical fanatics caught up in a maelstrom of self-aggrandisement. This was the gist of the media revelations. Questions were raised in Parliament but the Home Office pleaded ignorance as did the prison governors and Mengle was made the scapegoat. He issued a brief statement in his defence about advancing the knowledge of mankind. He was of course promoted to oversee an asylum for those unfortunate to be certified insane.

CHAPTER 16

After the white-washing Home Office exercise regarding the Sanatorium's clandestine research programme, the facility was transformed into a convalescence facility for prisoners who had undergone surgery at a civilian hospital. The operating theatre was closed down, the band of cowboy neurologists decamped to the Amazon jungles to continue their good work. Old buck-toothed George Formby lookalike, the ear-syringe freak was promoted to chief of staff of the new order. It was now a functioning hospital that catered for ill and dying convicts. Rumour had it that every night, old buck-teeth would prowl the wards, torch in one hand, syringe in the other looking for volunteers to placate his fetish. Not a particle of wax was safe while he was on duty. Nevertheless the syringe-freaks promotion and the subsequent removal of the blackmailing sword of Damocles from the hands of the unbridled psychiatrist engendered a huge sigh of relief from the four hundred lifers.

A couple of ex-Broadmoor inmates appeared on the wings during this period. Alan P., a lunatic of the highest order and as mad as a hatter. The other, Bob Mawdsley, a killer from Liverpool, sentenced to life for a brutal slaying and certified as insane, thus carted off to Broadmoor. He was caged within this asylum for many years when he, along with another felon decided on taking another patient hostage in order to be removed from the institution. After a few days they decapitated the hostage, Bob was deemed to be compos mentis, resulting in his relocation to the kingdom of Wakefield.

Alan P. was in his late twenties, bloated body and face from years of prescribed liquid narcotics, he had slaughtered a relative for which he was given a life term and had spent a third of his life in Broadmoor. He was truly fucked-up in the head. He pestered me for help in getting him out. He believed he was a hit-man for the mob, obsessed with gangsters and gang-land killers. Always immaculately attired, he was employed in the prison laundry; he wore a clean starched shirt and tie each and every day.

Bob Mawdsley was a tall, gangly big-boned man in his early thirties; he too suffered physical damage from prescribed narcotic abuse. He was an extremely dangerous individual as his antecedents depicted. Bob had been involved previously in two particularly gruesome murders. I worked as a gym orderly, assisting the Screw instructors in the training and remedial classes, when Bob was placed on morning remedial classes to rebuild the muscle depletion he suffered at Broadmoor. Being from Liverpool, I often conversed with him during the remedial classes and I realised then that he was a walking time bomb; how the trained shrinks failed to spot this aberration defies logic. He displayed a pathological hatred for sex-offenders, cursing them whenever one happened to stray into his space.

Observing the predatory nature of Bob as he stalked about the prison tiers was comparable to watching a caged wild animal in a zoo; he couldn't relax, he was always darting about, rarely indulging in the many wing activities. A proverbial cat on a hot tin roof. Wakefield's regime was proving difficult to hack for this particular killer.

I was relaxing in my cell playing cards with a couple of friends when there was a knock on the door; I yelled out for the intruder to enter; it was Bob. He apologised for interrupting the game but wanted me to draft a petition asking the authorities to send him back to Broadmoor.

"You sure mate? Asking to be sent back there isn't the wisest of career moves," I advised the ticking bomb.

"Fuckin' better than here. I had a bird who I used to grope at the Friday night dances. Fuck-all like that in this poxy place," he declared intently, still standing in the door jamb his eyes staring off to some distant planet.

"Give me the drift of it tomorrow mate and I'll knock something up for you," I replied, hoping this would appease the disgruntled nut.

"That's sound mate. See you in the gym then," he said, a smile on his face. He turned to dart off along the tier.

"Is that guy for real," asked Paddy Mac, one of the card school, shaking his head in disbelief at Bob's attitude.

"He's round the fuckin' bend. The guy's got serious issues. I seem to attract these crackpots. Must think I'm the good fuckin' shepherd," I stated, somewhat aggrieved at Bob pestering me with his problem.

"Blank him, mate. He's a fuckin' headache," Paddy said, aware of the hassle that mixing with oddballs can create within the close confines of a jail. "Don't worry - he will be kept at arm's length," I replied, agreeing with Paddy's assessment of the volatile Bob.

On the wing in which we were housed there were about four or five known sex-offenders scattered about the tiers like prickly weeds. They invariably kept to themselves, were shunned by most of the natives, nearly all had been assaulted during their incarceration. These beasts received a degree of protection from the authorities; they seldom moved from the sanctuary of their cells. I bumped into one of these abominations one day who claimed that I assaulted him, an allegation I repudiated but nevertheless it cost me a spell in segregation and two weeks loss of remission. I seldom ever spotted these creatures although it was known they lurked about in the shadowy zones. Bob was forever ranting about them.

A month or so after Bob handed in his petition for a relocation back to the Friday Night Ball and groping sessions, he was told his plea was refused. He ranted and raved at the assistant governor who had Bob removed to the segregation unit for a cooling off period. When he came back from isolation he returned to remedial classes looking calm and fully in control of his emotions. He told me that they're going to be sorry for not sending him back to Broadmoor. I put the statement down to bluster born out of frustration. He repeated the same statement to Paddy Mac.

Bob was designated employment in the metal fabrication factory, not a particularly popular choice of work. The factory manufactured metal cell doors for most of the prisons in the U.K. Steven a lifer who gambled on the horses was placing a bet. He worked with Bob producing steel doors and revealed that Bob had snaffled a broken length of a serrated saw and fashioned it into a gruesome looking blade. I took his bet and thanked him for his tit-bit of gossip. Normally when a convict arms himself, he is having problems that pose a threat to his well-being but as far as I was aware, the loon had no hassle with anybody of note who could threaten his existence.

Paddy bustled into my cell having had a brief encounter with the stalking predator on the stairwell. He told Paddy that he was making a death list of nonces he intended to kill to further his bizarre desire to be extradited to the comforts of the madhouse. He asked Paddy if there was anybody he wanted killing. Paddy pondered for a moment, then jokingly named a nonce case who resided on our landing, Bob whipped out his exercise book and commenced to scribble the name down. "Can you believe this crazy fucker? He's making a list of fuckin' nonces to do in. I asked him to do that slimy bastard Boris. He says don't worry - he'll go first. He opens a pillow slip he's holding to show me this fuckin' blade; it was like a fuckin' sword." Paddy rubbed his meaty paws together gleefully as he relished the thought of Bob transforming himself into a reincarnation of the Grim Reaper.

"Ignore the nut. I think he's fuckin' at it, playing a role to get the Screws to pounce on him, find his home-made sword then fuck him off," I suggested, because of his swaggering declaration of murderous intent.

If the Screws pick up on this behaviour the culprit is usually swooped on before any damage is done. I didn't realise that the Screws assigned to patrol the wing were all complacent drunks, ignorant of life on the tiers. A herd of elephants stampeding up and down the landings wouldn't have stirred these myopic sloths from their slumberous disposition. Bob's offer to execute nonces on request was a well discussed secret amongst all the criminal element on the tier, the Screws were lost in an alcoholic haze, utterly unaware of the serial killer walking by using a pillowslip as a scabbard to conceal a gruesome weapon.

I was standing outside my cell watching the carnival unfold in the night time association zones, hustling bustling convicts shifting positions, a cacophony of sounds from the numerous activities mingling together like a symphony composed in Hell. Paddy brought up a fresh flask of hot coffee and a couple of steak sandwiches, we retreated into the sanctuary of my cell, closing the door to shut out the constant din percolating amongst the tribe below.

"I seen the loon hanging about the showers, he said he's waiting for one of the names on his fuckin' death list to step in, he's gonna start killing the bastards," Paddy blurted out, recounting the previous encounter with the stalking poacher on the prowl for prey.

I still disbelieved Bob's intentions. He certainly looked suspicious as he stood alone in the shadows carrying his gruesome killing tools in a pillowslip.

"I think the guys at the bollocks. Fuck 'em let the nuts get on with their lunacy," I replied, bored with the turbulent troubles and behaviour difficulties of the misfits roaming the cell block.

Nothing happened that night adding credence to my suspicion that Bob's abnormal murder plot was a deliberate sham, a ploy which if discovered could force the hand of the authorities into complying with Bob's wishes. All prisoners were banged up alive and accounted for that night. Saturday morning I ritually made myself toast and coffee before going to work in the gym. I looked forward to this particular weekly routine as it gave me the opportunity to rendezvous with the many Liverpool inmates scattered about the other wings. We caught up on the gossip from the home town, who had been arrested, whose wife had eloped taking the family jewels, who had committed a daring criminal coup. It was a time to reminisce about the good times, the birds we seduced, the clubs and pubs we drank and cavorted about in from dusk to dawn. These weekly sessions would fly by providing a refreshing couple of hours with people I could identify with and share a common bond.

I got back to the wing roughly three-quarters of an hour prior to lunchtime lock-up when all the inmates are head counted. After picking up a tray of food from the hot-plate, I strode up the back stairwell on the way to my cell and as I arrived on my landing I spotted Bob leaning on the hand rail, pillow slip in hand; as I approached he turned to engage me in a chat. I noticed bright red stains dotted about the pillow case but didn't immediately compute the significance of these stains.

"OK mate. Listen…, I've done two," Bob revealed in a calm matter of fact tone, still leaning on the hand rail.

"Fuck off Bob," I replied, believing he was fantasising.

I turned and was about to head for my cell when he tugged at my jacket.

"I've done that nonce bastard Darwood and the other slimy

prick Darnley.

Come on I'll show you." he was eager to substantiate his claim.

I still wasn't convinced of the gravity of his confession so I thought I would humour him and tag along whilst keeping a wary eye on his pillowslip concealing the blade.

We descended one flight of stairs to the next landing and Bob made straight for the cell of inmate Darwood; I followed a pace or two behind him. The cell door was slightly ajar. Bob entered and I stayed in the doorway scanning the interior; at first glance nothing appeared amiss. "Piss off Bob," I exclaimed and was about to retreat when he cried out.

"Look, he's under fuckin' here," he lifted the mattress up off the bed to reveal the almost decapitated corpse of inmate Darwood lying in a thick puddle of blood under his own bed.

I lingered for a moment taking in the macabre scene. The corpse's head hanging grotesquely away from the torso revealing a huge gaping hole where the neck once was.

The madman giggled as he placed the mattress back in place. Before I departed the crime scene I observed blood stained towels and blood stained prison clothes piled in a corner of the cell.

"Fuck me Bob you've done the business," I exclaimed, patronising the smiling assassin and eager to extradite myself from his presence.

"I told you, these bastards are gonna be sorry for fuckin' me about," he ranted as we beat a hasty retreat from the scene.

Before I could rid myself of his unwanted company, he insisted that I see the body of his second victim, Darnley.

I let curiosity get the better and trailed behind him as he sped towards his last act of murder. Again I stood in the door jamb as Bob returned to the death scene, revelling in disclosing his deadly handiwork. He had slain this victim by thrusting the serrated blade forcefully into the right ear bursting the eardrum before entering the brain. As he removed the gruesome weapon, bodily matter mixed with blood spurted out to stain the cell walls. These details were revealed to me by this ice cold psychopath as he lifted the blanket off Darnley's corpse laying down on his bed as if in a deep sleep.

I quickly scrambled away from the second murder scene, Bob in tow, mouthing off how he easily disposed of his first victim by garrotting him with a home-made killing tool using a guitar string and two pieces of wood. I detoured to Paddy's cell leaving Bob to his murderous rampage. As I headed off in the opposite direction, he bawled out to my retreating back that Boris was next on his list. He sauntered off happy as Larry whistling a Beatles song as he hunted down his next victim.

Paddy was virtually frothing at the mouth when I eventually caught up with him. Apparently Bob had disposed of his victims earlier in the morning in between conducting selected faces on a grand tour of the murder scenes. He was trying his damnedest to increase the body count.

Paddy and another pal of ours had visited the sites of these horrendous acts of butchery guided by Bob who described in detail the techniques he employed to gain the confidence of the dead men. They were both lured to their demise by a simple offer of a pornographic magazine. Bob went to their respective cells and asked them to gaze through the pages of the grubby material. The unsuspecting reader fell for the killers opening gambit to their eternal and final regret as they were struck down violently by a maniac with no motive other than to be transferred back to Bedlam by brutally ending the life of the two penal pariahs.

The lunchtime lock-up and subsequent head-count was under way. I stood outside my cell observing the drama unfolding on the tier below, a Screw had peeped into Darwood's cell, thought he was dawdling somewhere and began yelling his name out loudly, most of the block were banged up when Bob called to the searching Screw to take a look under the missing man's bed and the naive officer duly obliged. Seconds later he came staggering out vomiting. Other officers reacted by dashing to his aid thinking he had been assaulted; chaos erupted when they discovered the corpse.

Meanwhile Bob, who had alerted the officer to the whereabouts of the corpse, strolled nonchalantly towards the wing offices disregarding screams for him to return to his cell. A committee awaited the grinning psychopath as he approached the office pillowslip in hand. He passed it to a senior officer saying take a look in there. The man peeked inside glimpsing the weapons of the homicides, a garrotte and a blade stained with the blood and bodily fluids of both victims. His face turned snow white and he became transfixed to the spot unable to talk. Bob chanted out loudly, a broad smile upon his face, "I told you that you'd be fuckin' sorry."

He was jumped on by a mob of officers, restrained then carted off to the isolation unit never to be seen again.

After the discovery of the two stiffs, the prison was on total lock-down. The wing became a crime scene with the local constabulary called in to investigate an open and shut case of homicide. Forensic teams were bustling about sifting through the evidence whilst photographing the gory details of the offence. It took two full days before normal routine resumed and the restless natives emerged from their enforced hibernation, chattering about the crimes of Broadmoor Bob. The plot he conjured up in order to return to the dancing sessions at the Friday night discos resulted in two corpses in the morgue, a plot conceived in sheer madness and devoid of a modicum of rationality.

Bob was arraigned on the two counts of murder and a

futile defence was mounted on the grounds of diminished responsibility. Even though it was patently evident, even to a wild savage from the jungles of the Amazon, that Bob was stark raving mad, the prosecution found psychiatrists prepared to testify that Bob was fit to stand trial. A conclusion endorsed by a wise old red-robed judge. The due process of the law illuminated the heavens by deeming this mad man sane leading to a subsequent trial and the inevitable guilty verdict. Bob added another two life sentences to his tally making a grand total of four consecutive life terms. It was decided that he had now forfeited his right to ever mingle in a penal population again, a specially constructed strong room was constructed deep within the bowels of the prison which would house Bob for the remainder of his oxygen inhaling days.

He brutally cut down these pariahs for no other reason than to be relocated back to his previous place of incarceration where he had access to female patients once a week. He bore no malice towards these men other than the nature of the indictment that initially incarcerated them. They were selected for death randomly, along with a number of other penal pariahs who, but for the luck of Lucifer, could have joined their outcast brethren on a slab in the morgue.

Alan P, the well-dressed fantasizer, who shared the same asylum roots as Bob, confessed to being party to the homicide of the two nonce cases. He babbled on to me and Paddy that he strangled the deceased then battered their brains in. I fobbed the nut off by telling him to inform the governor and he would get his name in the paper. He immediately flew down to the wing office making a statement to the governor about his role in the butchery. He was marched off to isolation waving to the inmate onlookers, a broad smile on his deluded face, shouting, "I whacked them out."

A few days later he re-emerged from the unit, his bogus

confession being tossed out by the police. After a brief interview, they realised his detailed account was fictional and that they were dealing with a totally unstable nut. He continued boasting that he done the business along with his partner Bob. The serial confessor had inherited a considerable sum of money from the estate of a departed relative which encouraged him to change his name by deed poll to a double-barrelled aristocratic nom de plume. He adopted the new moniker, scribbling it on the identity card posted outside his prison cell. However, everybody including the Screws still used his birth title when conversing with the crackpot.

Dental treatment is organised on a monthly basis by application through the wing office allowing the applicant to be put on an appointment list. I arrived at the treatment room at the end of the wing along with a number of other convicts including Alan the confessor, dressed immaculately for the occasion. A few patients had been dealt with when the Screw in attendance called in Alan P. for treatment. The nut blanked the call, sitting there staring off into space, his arms folded tightly across his chest. His name was repeated several times stating that he was next in line. He ignored the invitation and turning to me and a few other inmates, he enquired if we knew anybody by that name. He then replied to the Screw who was glaring impatiently at him, "Nobody with that name here boss."

He refused to respond to his name and sat rigidly looking up at the ceiling. A deadlock situation arose; neither of the antagonists would budge and it ended with Alan P. returning to his cell without receiving the dental work that he had applied for.

That was the last of the many bizarre memories I have of this mansion of monsters.

CHAPTER 17

I was disheartened by my removal from the educational programme because of the opportunity it provided to mix with free-thinking tutors who attended the facility on a daily basis; people whose attitudes were not corroded by the demands of a grotesque society. I was given light duties as a cleaner on the wing, a job I loathed, swilling the latrines out each morning. I paid a lifer to do it for me while I went to the gym and played badminton. Escape became a more significant factor as I loitered on the wing bored off my cake.

The hair brained plot hatched in alcohol seemed the best out of the numerous escape strategies bouncing about the prison. Eddy, a Republican lifer, buried for all eternity by a red-robed philanthropist, declared he had a source that may be able to supply us with a pair of wire cutters, an important tool to effect a swift break out of the compound. An inmate had a pipe-line into the jail, he was prepared to utilise this source as long as he was invited to participate in any escapes that were on the go. His request was agreed to and the plan was now in motion.

Ken, the Casanova lifer had managed to corrupt a dowdy female frump who attended the Bible reading classes organised by the prison chaplain. These weekly religious soirées were part of penal culture, an input from the church to justify their role as a positive influence in cleansing the souls of the multitude of jailhouse sinners who were clinging to delusional threads. A group of civilian Christian stalwarts from a local church had been gracing these events for many years, about four or five middle aged maidens regularly attended accompanied by a few masculine martyrs who believed they were doing God's work.

Ken, who had been convicted of a catalogue of particularly heinous crimes, was the very epitome of social etiquette as he fluttered about the guests passing them tea and complimenting the female frumps on their well-groomed hair, their perfume, their clothes; he acted the perfect gentleman as he fussed about in the interlude before the Bible-reading mob got down to business. A Screw was supposed to oversee the class to ensure there was no fraternising but after many years of Biblical guff the Screw would retreat to the rear of the chapel with a flask of fortified tea and a selection of Men Only magazines - complacency enveloped his academic head. Ken took full advantage of the Screw's apathy using an armoury of flattery to woo one of the vulnerable wall-flowers. He selected what he considered the most hideous and emotionally insecure of the maidens, plying her with gracious verbal bouquets, then slipping her a love letter with tea and biscuits. The fragile maiden succumbed to the killer's charm by replying to Ken's letters of love. Ken had truly bowled the maiden over enabling him to exploit the situation, first by small requests for cigarettes then half bottles of spirits and a few of life's other little luxuries were presented to him by the gullible fool.

Ken's deceitful protestations of eternal love entangled the perennial wall-flower in an inextricable web. This grossly overweight frump, who resembled a fish swallowing pelican with layers of excess fat tissue dangling from her chin had put herself in a position where if things backfired she could find herself behind bars serving a sentence. One of the Casanova's gambits was to propose marriage, painting a picture of romantic adventures with bouts of marathon love making when he is released in the future. Ken was never going to be released, he had spent almost two decades in jail and had recently had his review date put back for at least ten years. Ken was doomed.

To get the holy frump to smuggle a pair of wire cutters inside the prison, Casanova Ken inveigled her with an elaborate lie that he could slip out of the prison unnoticed by cutting through a flimsy perimeter fence, scale the walls, consummate their love then slip back in before unlock. The smitten pelican-necked virgin swallowed his lies as quick as her feathered lookalike ate fish and agreed to smuggle the tool in. Ken danced into the bath-house after the Bible-bashing indoctrination enclave had finished for the night. He was shaking his pony-tailed mane in jubilation because the fixated wench had acceded to his sweet-talking promises and agreed to bring the cutters with her to the following Bible reading class. The heartless gigolo was mocking the poor besotted maiden who risked her very liberty by smuggling illicit goods to him. He crowed that she could smuggle a Sherman tank in under all those layers of lard, such was the fickleness of this student of the Bible.

Every Saturday afternoon, an inter-wing football match took place on the compound and most of the inmates would come out to observe the game. Also, the fitness fanatics would jog around the perimeter; a number of ramblers would stroll briskly to exercise their lungs all making for a bustling ambience that was difficult to monitor. An eighteen-foot mesh fence fitted with tremblers which alerted the prison security nerve centre if breached encompassed the compound. On match days, the alarm system was switched off because of the ball smashing into it and the number of prisoners that often rested against the security fence. This weakness had been absorbed by Eddy the Republican but utilising the information to an advantage had been a problem until this Kamikaze plot. Behind the fencing, approximately four metres away, stood a six metre high wall; over the wall was a main road often busy with traffic. The plan was to cut the fence and scale the wall landing in the roadway where it was every man for himself.

Scaling the wall could be achieved with a grappling hook and rope; there was a steel lighting post jutting from the top of the wall which would be ideal for attaching the hook. Speed was of the essence if this escape was to succeed as was the recruitment of more eager escapees deployed to ward off the Screws who would be on their toes once the fence was breached and the grappling iron tossed at the wall.

A notorious escapee who had bust out of local prisons and almost escaped from Gartree, a maximum-security prison with identical escape-proof obstacles as Hull, was recruited to the scheme. He fashioned a grappling hook using metal from the prison bed-frames. This could be concealed in two segments and smuggled onto the compound. Rope to fasten onto the hook was not a problem, there were plenty of short lengths in the workshops. Everything appeared to be on schedule and it was up to the pony-tailed charmer to deliver the cutters.

Casanova got dressed in his finest threads, shoes bulled up, hair shampooed and well brushed back into his familiar pony-tail, drenched himself in borrowed after-shave, then sauntered off to rendezvous with the besotted frump. The two Irishmen where sitting swigging beer when I caught up with them to discuss the plot which relied on the return of Ken with a vital ingredient in the escape conspiracy. It was decided that I would secrete the cutters in a sewage drain wrapped in waterproof polythene. I would retrieve them on the morning of the mass breakout. If the plan worked and we managed to get over the wall we concluded that we would commandeer a car then drive about a mile from the prison, abandon that car, then hijack another vehicle taking the occupant with us. That was the immediate action we would embark on to escape the area.

I had made arrangements for Micky, a loyal friend, to await

a call from me to a phone-box in close proximity to Hull; he would then pick us up and take us to Liverpool. A safe house was sorted for the three of us where we would squat until safe passage could be arranged to surreptitiously export us to Southern Ireland where we would find freedom.

A passport and a change of identity would be available from the Irishmen's colleagues. That was the dream, a dream that boosted my morale and heightened the tension, sending the blood pulsating through my body in anticipation of a band of brigands steaming out of the compound. Subliminal thoughts about the escape eradicated all doubts concerning risks or failure.

Ken appeared with the cutters stuffed down his pants; he was ecstatic as if he had discovered the secret of eternal life, buzzing about the cell unable to keep still with excitement causing Eddy to admonish him. Cool heads were required, not the antics of Casanova Ken whose puerile behaviour might attract the attention of the authorities. I took possession of the implements which the pelican had wrapped inside a pair of her oversized knickers for the pleasure of her paramour, who extracted the cutters then proceeded to compare the underwear to a parachute, further ridiculing the exploited lass.

I advised Ken that if things come out on top, he should protect the identity of the Pelican as she had put herself in the frame to be prosecuted. The killer agreed to the suggestion, swearing an oath on the souls of his victims, a testimony I found rather weird when it was uttered. It should have alerted me that Ken was unstable and not capable of retaining his own counsel. Casanova and the five Bible bashing frumps had got lost in a mist of social inaccessibility; they were life's pariahs, shunned because of physical abnormalities or deep-rooted psychological deficiencies. Visiting a jailhouse, indulging in group therapy by pouring over Biblical fictional fables is itself abnormal behaviour for free-world citizens but they cling to the absurd notion that they are somehow doing God's work, when in reality they are preening their own feathers by substituting their miserable and lonely lifestyles for penal Bible readings. Ken and his ilk could not give a damn for the Bible or for that matter, any other human being. The class provided them with a momentary refuge from loneliness and from their wretched miserable lives. Ken had never shed a tear over any of his victims or displayed a vestige of remorse yet he had been attending the religious class for five years. The class was a gathering enclave for lonely hearts. Religion was the excuse, these misfits would attend weekly even if the syllabus was brass polishing.

Mid-week, we met to discuss the finer details of the crash out; the grappling hook had been prepared, several lengths of rope had been fashioned with knots for easier grip when ascending. Approximately ten determined men were involved in the plot all aware that a level of violence may have to be used to deter the first Screws from thwarting the escape and also that once the breakout is underway, other prisoners will take advantage of the situation by dashing for the wall too. Speed was essential if the plot were to succeed.

Jail society drifts along on a river of rumour and whispers. Amid the gossiping cults are the feeble domestic murderers who are estranged from the hard-core criminal elements. They have different attitude and values; they mix with other crimes-of-passion natives who share similar beliefs and ideologies. They have perpetrated a one-off crime by killing a promiscuous wife who wanted a divorce or strangled a lover who had jilted them. By the very nature of their criminal act, they were deemed to have weak characteristics and were more or less avoided by the general jailhouse population. Only the naive would take a domestic killer into their confidence. These creatures identify with the authorities and not the convict, they are invariably enlisted to work in the offices with civilian staff or in the officer's mess.

Thursday night, two days before the day of reckoning, Ken approached a fellow lifer, a domestic killer who strangled his wife because she was fornicating with his mate while he was playing darts in the local pub. He gives the strangler his most treasured possession, George a talking budgie, telling his confidante to take good care of the bird. The confused prisoner asked Ken why he's giving the budgie away as he knew that Ken must have formed a bond with George, his feathered friend. Unstable, bird-loving Ken then proceeds to divulge details of the escape plot, revealing the names of the main protagonists to the flabbergasted strangler who didn't consider himself a villain but a law abiding member of the free-world community. The new owner of the talking budgie immediately reports the plot to the wing governor, who responds by putting wheels into motion to torpedo our escape plan.

Friday morning six a.m. my door bursts open and a squad of grim-faced Screws confront me.

"Out of bed. You're leaving. Hurry up," an officer ordered in a gruff aggressive voice.

I glanced at my watch and realised that we'd been compromised; I didn't need an explanation from this band of androids.

"What's the problem Pop-eye?" I enquired of the muscle-bound Screw, who stood spread-legged in front of me with his shirt sleeves rolled up revealing his steroid induced biceps.

"You know the problem wise guy. Just grab your gear. You can get a wash in reception," he snarled impatiently at me. I grinned as I deliberately took my time which infuriated the muscle-bound mutant.

Delroy, whose cell was beneath mine could hear the commotion and began shouting out of his door in a booming voice threatening to knock out muscles. The wing aroused by Delroy began screaming and banging loudly on their doors. Muscles immediately changed his stance begging me to please hurry up; he explained that he was only obeying orders and didn't want to offend anyone. I departed from the wing escorted by four Screws who led me to the prison reception where they waited while I had a shower and then locked me in a steel cage. The reception administrator gave me a coffee, whispering to me that I was being extradited for good order and discipline; the two Irishmen have already passed through. I thanked him for the news. He quickly darted off as the jangling of keys rattling in a lock notified him that officials were approaching. It was the Security Chief and the governor, I was hustled into an office where this pair of professional penologists attempted to question me.

"You're in serious trouble Smith. You and a group of prisoners were prepared to use violence against my officers to effect an escape from lawful custody. This is a grave offence - it constitutes mutiny and is punishable by a severe custodial sentence." The governor droned on parrot fashion quoting rules and prison articles I had transgressed. I stared up at the ceiling awaiting the friendly approach from the chief.

"Look Scouse, there's no need for you to suffer, just tell me where the cutters are hidden and the name of the individual who smuggled them in. You help us and I'll make sure no further charges will be levelled against you. Instead of going on a merry-go-around, I'll send you to another long-term complex." The chief spoke in a calm avuncular voice his eyes dancing about his friendly smiling face.

"I haven't a clue what you are both rambling on about. I've

never contemplated an escape," I replied to the benevolent thespians as calm and two faced as they both were as they addressed me.

"Listen you lying scoundrel, everything that occurs inside these walls gets reported back to me. I know what you and your Republican friends were plotting in my jail. I told you before that you are too clever for your own good. I will make sure you spend the next year in the worst segregation units in the country." The governor cried out in frustration, slapping his pampered hand on the desk.

"Come on Scouse, a few details about the cutters and the name of the smuggler and I give you my word that you'll be looked after, otherwise you're in for a hard time." The helpful chief spouted, attempting to cajole me into digging my own grave. I paused for a minute as if I was considering his invitation to cooperate. The amateur detective held his breath in anticipation.

"Chief, I'll be honest with you, I heard there was a plot afoot but it didn't involve me. I heard that Muscles (the steroid headed security Screw) was having a homosexual affair with one of the prisoners. I believe the prisoner was blackmailing him into bringing all kinds of contraband in. I heard a snippet of gossip that he was supplying the stuff for the escape," I lied as convincingly as possible without grinning. The pair of them glared at me with disgust, the governor wanted to put me on the rack and torture the life out of me.

"Take this reprobate out of my sight," the governor roared to the chief who hastily dispatched me into the steel strong box. I could hear the governor muttering to himself in the distance.

"You are a very silly man. You could have done this the easy way," the not-so-friendly chief intimated as he locked me in.

"Fuck-off and stop reading detective manuals. Dickhead," I

yelled as I sank down to confront the rough road ahead."

I was unlocked, then taken to a waiting prison van which sped out of the gates where two police cars greeted us, lights flashing, sirens blaring, they flew down the road scaring the living daylights out of pedestrians and motorists alike. Hull soon vanished to be dispatched to my memory. I didn't know until later how the plot was compromised but my original instinct was to assign the blame to Ken, he was a sadistic unstable killer with no sense of in-house security. The amateur sleuth, by asking about the cutters, had made it obvious that he had gotten the information from a prisoner but not any of the main players otherwise he wouldn't be pumping me for information about the identity of the smuggler or the whereabouts of the implement. I guessed the leak had sprung from the lips of the Casanova convict who had unwittingly bragged to one of his misfit pals. I got the full breakdown a year or so later when I caught up with some of the escape committee at Long Lartin Prison. A talking budgie brought the house down. Casanova never divulged the identity of the pelican as the contraband conduit and he remained at Hull as far as I know. His name never cropped up anywhere in the gulags after the fact. I wasn't concerned about any legal implications that might be indictable relating to the aborted escape plot, despite the bluster puffed out by the governor, however I did expect a vindictive reprisal in the form of isolation.

I eventually arrived at H.M.P. Leeds - a local transit camp crammed with short-term felons, a notorious filthy hole at the time which was controlled by a thuggish regime who ruled by fear. I was dumped straight into the segregation dungeon, placed in a cell containing a bed with half a mattress, a battered cardboard table and a reinforced cardboard chair. It was filthy with urine and excrement stains on the floors and walls - a typical punishment cell in this satanic pit overseen by public servants who were paid to provide humane and proper care of the inhabitants. Four hours later the door opened to reveal a trolley guarded by two burly cavemen, a metal tray with food splashed in a heap was presented to me.

"Dinner!" one of the Neanderthals grunted staring at my face in an overt intimidatory manner. Antagonism oozed from every pore of the two brutes as they stood in attack mode, daring me to respond.

"That food looks delicious," I commented sarcastically as I accepted the tray of slops.

"Make the most of it you Scouse bastard," one of the thugs blurted aggressively.

I poked at the food with a plastic fork; the bastards had poured custard over the potatoes and a small piece of meat. I looked at the walls in despair as I realised this would be a severe test of my resolve. I began to pace up and down the cell, a ubiquitous odour of urine assaulting my senses. Soon the rhythm allowed me to drift off and wander in past visions of freedom.

Every day in solitary a governor is theoretically obliged to check on the welfare of those lodged in isolation; it was a few days before I had the privilege of seeing the despot in charge of this pigsty.

"Name and number to the governor!" A senior officer yelled loudly at me as he opened the door, the governor standing there flanked by two slashed peaked Gestapo clones.

"Elvis Presley 064," I barked back sarcastically to the role-playing androids. The governor smirked looking me up and down with contempt.

"Any complaints Smith?" he requested hypocritically, his two body guards eyeballing me as if I were filth.

"None whatsoever boss. One of the best hotels I have stayed in. Could you provide me with a bucket of hot soapy water and a mop so I can clean up the mess left by the previous tenant?" I asked in response to his mask of insincerity.

"Officer, make sure this man gets ample hot water to clean his room," he barked as the door was slammed in my face.

I spent four weeks bogged down in this cesspit, struggling with daily confrontations posed by meat-brained ruffians who were spoiling for a fight. One morning I was guided to reception and moved to Strangeways prison in Manchester, where I was again subjected to the same regimen, segregation unit accompanied by a symphony of intimidation orchestrated by chest-beating thugs.

Stangeways, unlike Leeds was spotlessly clean, the unit's floors were scrubbed and polished daily; each cell was inspected every morning by a hygiene conscious officer who ensured the occupant was provided with the essential equipment to keep it clean. Woe betide the scruffy idlers who failed to meet the hygiene standards, a good slapping would be dished out to the culprit. I could live with the hassle as long as there was no filth and stench contaminating the airflow. A month of repetitive torment swiftly passed when I assume the expert investigation into the escape plot was concluded without any evidence to indict me, so I was given the benefit of the doubt and transhipped to Long Lartin prison near Evesham.

CHAPTER 18

Long Lartin is located in the Vale of Evesham, constructed in the countryside; within its secure escape-proof walls were large playing fields, trees dotted about growing in grassy knolls; it was in stark contrast to the concrete tombs I had dwelt in during the previous few years. A feeling of relief hit me as I landed in the reception area where cheerful Screws welcomed me with fresh coffee, exchanging banter about football, treating me with respect, doing what they were paid to do, a far cry from the confrontational meat-heads stamping through the short-term transit camps. A security Screw popped in explaining the relaxed atmosphere of the jail with modern facilities.

"Toe the line and you will have no problems from the staff. We are here to help you through your sentence, not to make it more difficult for you," he declared in a friendly voice. I thought I had been transported to a holiday camp, such was the bonhomie extended to me. I wondered if a porter was waiting to carry my baggage as he showed the way to the cell block.

I was familiar with a good few of the natives, some had been ebbing and flowing about the gulag system for decades, others I recognised from the streets of Liverpool. I was located in a cell adjacent to Errol Hinksman who had shared the security cage with me in Risley. The passing years had treated him kindly - he exuded health and vitality. Deprived of access to the hedonistic lifestyle of loose women and vintage wines had certainly preserved his appearance. He was a master Chef. Having spent a couple of years in this particular calaboose, he established himself with all the covert conduits to ensure he ate well; that night we dined on tuna steaks seasoned with lemon and garlic served on a bed of Indian rice. He managed to bribe a Screw to bring in a bottle of Chablis.

A man of many means was the deep thinking Errol. He had owned a top-class restaurant in Sydney where he learnt his culinary skills, he could make cabbage taste delicious with a mixture of exotic spices.

Vinnie dawdled here prior to the Miracle of Emancipation, with his Houdini escape manoeuvre that sprung him to freedom almost as quick as the torpedoes ordered by Thatcher sank the Belgrano. Errol fed me the scandal as he had befriended Vinnie during his weekend break here. According to his analysis, Vinnie had corrupted a few Screws as well as a high-ranking civil servant who doctored his parole application. He gathered that a considerable sum of money exchanged hands and the person who brokered the deal was none other than Fatso who had been visiting Vinnie on a regular basis. A blip registered on my innate radar at this snippet of gossip. Bending a governor or a parole officer was a fabrication that didn't sit easy with me at the time; other skulduggery was afoot that was not declarable to an outsider. I made a mental note with the intention of checking its veracity at a later date. Fairy-tales abound amongst the criminal fraternity.

A decade or so later when I was able to calculate the historical chain of events that evolved around these soot-juggling foxes, I believe that Fatso's role in infiltrating organised crime mobs became a blueprint utilised by all the enforcement agencies in the United Kingdom. He was a pioneer - these sorcerers were encouraged to ply their illegal activities more so when narcotics superseded robbery, theft and extortion as the main source of income for organised crime. Webs of deception were spun to safeguard the informant who was given a licence to engage in narcotic importation and distribution. As their influence and status as crime lords blossomed so did the amount of bodies that were being incarcerated inside prison cells. They became the main weapon employed by the law enforcers in the prosecution of drug felons.

A popular ruse in recruiting high profile traffickers to the undercover squads was to arrest them red-handed with a consignment of narcotics, then offer them immunity for the offence if they become an informant. A scenario would be created by the police to justify the new recruit's escape from justice with the magical wand of technicalities. They will be allowed to walk free from a court-room or police station on a technicality in spite of overwhelming evidence. Of course, some of the undercover squad don't even get as far as the police station, nor do they ever sit in a courthouse dock; they roll-over soon as they see a uniform shuffling up their path. They volunteer to cooperate quicker than a speeding bullet; a statement implicating friends, associates, cohorts, mothers, fathers and brothers will be deposited in the lap of startled officers who believe they are arresting a hard-core villain rather than a self-preservationist who cannot stop singing.

The technicality clause is really a euphemism for 'I am now a deep-rooted undercover cop'. It is widely suspected that some of the most successful of these sorcerers also receive a percentage of the street value of drugs recovered as the result of their treachery. Furthermore, money and assets seized also benefit the informant. Whenever a felon declares that charges were withdrawn on a technicality, you can wager your soul to Satan Himself that the miscreant has been recruited to the undercover squad. A squad founded on the experiences of Fat Sid, the original master of deceit and intrigue. A man who dictated policy to his handler and bossed inferior ranking officers. A profile accidentally discovered by a modern day archaeologist as he trawled through secret police files.

Errol's gossip planted a seed inside my brain that remained

dormant for many a day, a seed of suspicion that refused to disappear, niggling away like an infected tooth.

Adjusting to a variety of alien cultures that ferment in each different penal colony is a relatively simple task when your face is known by some of the other inmates. They are in a position to recommend the credibility of the newcomer. A stranger entering this environment will be snubbed, treated with suspicion and an element of hostility until their history is substantiated; then and only then are they accepted into the fold with access to the contraband conduits that flourish in maximum-security gulags. I had no such problems, most of my neighbourhood were behind bars. I followed the preliminary induction parade, chaired by amateur psychiatrists a sociologist and two prison officers, all guilty of squandering tax-payers money asking asinine questions. These people are superfluous to the system with their pitiful attempts to classify rogue humans into scientifically labelled specimens. I was duly processed after a couple of days wasted listening to these pseudo-intellects blowing their respective verbal trumpets. I fed them a distorted prognosis of my traumatised body which persuaded them to assign me to educational classes where I could complete the degree course I was already half way through. A feather in my penal cap by bamboozling the cabal of inquisitors into believing I was disabled due to all the bone implants in my arm and a bullet wound to my lung, thus blessing me with an easy servitude passage.

Unlike Hull and the notorious mansion of monsters, in Wakefield, the ratio of nomadic lifers to determinate sentence inhabitants was far less. This equated to a more stable environment easing the defensive paranoia climate that prevailed in other jailhouse societies over-populated with killers. Survival instincts, primed to maximum alert each waking day as you exited your cell and mingled with the herd of homicidal misfits, could be relaxed, allowing you to walk without having your eyeballs swivelling in their sockets searching for lunatics on the warpath. Long Lartin functioned on a policy of internal relaxation of restrictive practices. This encouraged an atmosphere of cordiality between the staff and prisoners whilst operating a high security escape-proof perimeter. It was the easiest institutional regime I had encountered on my penal odyssey, a holiday camp with razor wire fencing.

A large library was located at the centre of the jail overseen by Bob, a daydreaming officer. I often spent an hour or two studying there of a night, engaging Bob in conversation. As I could type, he asked me to work with him as a librarian. I accepted his proposal. Bob was heading for retirement after twenty years as a Screw having previously served in the armed forces. He was a polite, softly-spoken man who dwelt in a fantasy world. He continually boasted about his heroic escapades behind enemy lines where he captured leading Nazi-officers, gave them the third-degree prior to disposing of them with a single shot to the back of the head. I listened to his sagas for a while; they gradually became more expansive as time passed, especially his adventures as a major in the S.A.S. Instead of contradicting his fibs, I openly encouraged him to spin more lies, chipping in with his parachuting experiences, trying to assassinate Hitler. I realised he was delusional and he believed these ridiculous untruths; by catering to his aberration I ended up running the library with Bob's mind travelling around wartime Germany blowing up bridges and I had a free hand which I exploited to the full.

Each morning Bob would pick up two sacks of mail containing newspapers, magazines and books from the reception area and deliver them to the library. He was supposed to search and censor every item for contraband before distributing it to each wing. After a while, apathy set in and Bob entrusted me to sort the mail while he read wartime biographies and smoked his head off. I began by selecting low-profile prisoners and had books sent to them with money secreted inside. I intercepted these books without any hint of suspicion. I was flabbergasted at the ease of this breach of internal security.

I went up a notch sending in booze paraphernalia such as yeast and hops, again no problem. In those days inmates were not allowed a television in their cells. I had a book-sized portable television sent in using the same system. It flew in being delivered by the day-dreaming commando. I used to watch it in my cell after night-time lock-up. I never disclosed this smuggling route to anybody utilising it purely for luxuries. A secret shared becomes a rumour, then a snippet of gossip, then full blown public knowledge. Also, the desperado elements would be knocking on the door asking for guns or dynamite to be smuggled in, bringing Bob's house crumbling down and possibly increasing my jail term by another ten years or so. At the beginning of my sentence, these desperado tactics would have been a viable option but not now that I was approaching the half way mark. A slip through the bars without the use of fire power would still be grasped with both hands.

Errol often popped into the library ordering classical literary works. I would make him a coffee then indulge in a bit of banter with delusional Bob.

"Morning Major Bob, how's your shrapnel wounds?" Errol would comment sarcastically, a twinkle in his eye and a beaming smile lighting up his film-star looks.

Bob glanced up from his war literature returning Errol's greeting with a polite nod of his demented head.

"It's the back giving me grief today Errol, from too many night-time parachute jumps." Bob stood up grimacing as he rubbed his back dramatically.

This fable caused the smirk to widen on Errol s face as he

winked at me. A bout of piss-taking would commence with poor Bob unaware that we were amusing ourselves by inviting him to narrate a delusional fable or two.

"Get on to the war office Bob, see if you can claim some compensation for your battle injuries," Errol advised, his tongue firmly lodged in his pearly white teeth. I giggled as Bob took the bait.

"No can do. The S.A.S. is a volunteer elite group, a disclaimer is signed by all those who pass the stringent physical and mental trials from future compensatory action. We accept this criteria and are proud to do the dirty work for Queen and Country," he lied, as he spouted a rehearsed excerpt from one of his war books.

"Well Bob, considering the number of German officers you assassinated and the amount of bridges and tanks you blew up, you would expect the Government to take good care of you." Errol continued to bolster Bob's deluded image with a smirk enjoying the banter as I struggled to contain my laughter.

"We S.A.S. Are content with medals and proud to have done our duty. Did I tell you about the time we rescued top American brass from a fortress deep inside German held territory?" the day-dreaming Walter Mitty asked, his narrative juices flowing as he began to spin a tale straight out of a novel he had just finished reading.

"Didn't someone make a film about that Bob, I believe Richard Burton was in it?" The piss-taker's smirk turning into a laugh. I had to run out at this point engulfed in laughter as Bedlam Bob rambled on about another German invasion. I didn't want the fabricating fool to realise we were ridiculing him in the event it jeopardised my job in the library.

The comical Kiwi participated in these sessions at least once a week; Bob never caught on that he provided us with so much entertainment.

Ken, a homosexual Screw, was a relief officer when Bob had time off; he reminded me of an old time slapstick comedian. Ken couldn't keep still - he was hyperactive, whizzing about as if he'd swallowed an ounce of amphetamine. He informed me that Bob had never been to Germany in his life, he was in fact a private in the Royal Pioneer Corps, a regiment famous for digging ditches. Ken rubbished his workmate telling me he needs medical treatment. I had well deduced that fact without gay Ken endorsing the obvious. Ken didn't give a damn allowing me to sort out the mail. Complacency can penetrate the most sophisticated of systems. This loophole would never work in today's ultra-paranoid institutions.

Time galloped past, Bob was descending into a fantasy world which was causing concern amongst his fellow officers. I was gutted in case he might be forced to go on an extended leave with a disciplinary rule book freak stepping in to replace him. This could ultimately threaten the contraband pipe-line I had cultivated. He received a phone call one day and after the telephone-conversation was concluded, he turned to me and stated that it was the Foreign Office ringing to see if he could assist in the assassination of Colonel Gadaffi. I burst out laughing. He had completely lost the plot.

October, the twelfth after night bang-up, an almighty din broke out in the jailhouse, doors were struck incessantly, the natives were screaming and cheering as if it were New Year's Eve. I quickly made for the window to investigate the commotion, my initial inclination was that a break out was in progress. Voices could be heard yelling that they got that bastard - followed by an avalanche of cheers. Errol called my name.

"What the fucks going on mate?" I blurted out of my window.

"A bomb has just blown up those Tory pricks. It looks like they got Thatcher," he explained breathlessly as he fed me the news about the Brighton bombing.

The bomb planted by Republicans had sent the inmates delirious with delight. Thatcher was a reviled figure, absolutely loathed by the vast majority of convicts. Most would gladly contribute to her demise by driving a stake through her heart.

I retreated to my bunk, quickly tuning in the radio to catch the latest news bulletins on the bomb attack. A crescendo of howls coupled with cries of "they missed the slag" shattered the air around the prison buildings. To the utter dismay of most of the inmates Thatcher survived the attempt on her life. It's unfathomable to conceive that a Prime Minister could engender such widespread venom, 'Iron Pants' would certainly finish last in a prison popularity poll. One of the myriad reasons why this plutocratic disciple was reviled by prisoners the world over was her brutal intransigence during Bobby Sands' ultimate sacrifice when he starved himself to death in protest at being denied political status. A number of young Irishmen continued in the footsteps of Sands dying for a belief which a modicum of compassion from her money-mad administration could have resolved, bringing an end to the deadlock without the death of these precocious flowers of Irish youth. Future developments repudiated her obdurate edifice of cast-iron ruthlessness when The Good Friday agreement brought peace to the province, a solution that couldn't have been settled under the political ideology so prominent during Thatcher's reign.

On the yard, the day after the Brighton bombing, an uplifting buzz gripped the inmates as they debated the near miss on this symbol of working-class repression. Ninety-nine percent of jailhouse occupants hail from impoverished working-class backgrounds; most realised that the incumbent administration had little time for the under-privileged sectors of society. Insofar as they were concerned, we were being governed by a cabal of robber-barons, interested in amassing wealth for themselves and their wealthy backers. A revolutionary fervour flowed through the penal corridors at this juncture generating a sense of unified antipathy towards all things governmental. If only this antipathy could have been harnessed as a political force, maybe an alliance could have been forged with dissident factions creating a movement prepared to subvert the political status quo and overthrow the toffee nosed Tory limpets. Hatred festered and spread like an aggressive cancer.

An armed robber from my old neighbourhood popped up on the yard with a fifteen-year burden heaped on his shoulders.

A filthy informant betrayed him, the informant had no compunction for his dastardly deed, compounding his cowardly action by standing in the dock, bold as brass, testifying against him. The betrayed man, Jon Hasse along with another stand-up felon, Danny Vaughan, were the victims of a rampant homosexual and violent psychopath Roy Grantham. I knew all three men insofar as we shared a common attitude to increasing cash flow by steaming in on selected targets and help ourselves to the money. Prior to the Worcester catastrophe Grantham was running about with close associates of mine and a major crime was under consideration. I received an invitation to participate in the act. I rendezvoused with them on several occasions; Grantham would turn up speeding off his cake, high as a kite on amphetamine, exuding violence and looking every inch a psychopath. I never forgot his hands - they were huge strangling tools which he continually clenched and unclenched. I had reservations about taking part in a criminal enterprise with this ticking bomb. I foresaw blood and carnage if things turned sour.

A week before the planned robbery, Grantham raped a sixteen year old boy who lived in a multi-story block of flats. He terrorised the victim by hanging him over the tenth floor balcony by his ankles. Word of this unacceptable, vile violation of a boy reached the ears of the robbery conspirators who immediately abandoned the plot. Two of them caught up with the nut, pulling guns on him and threatening to blow his brains out if he ever showed his face again. He subsequently vanished from the Liverpool scene. So it came as a great surprise when I heard he had turned super-grass and pawned two staunch robbers. This vile specimen had been arrested on an unrelated act of sodomy, whilst bring interrogated by highly dignified and moral Christian police officers, Grantham offered to trade in some fellow robbery conspirators in exchange for immunity. A pact with this sodomising rapist, a man who had previously been committed to an insane asylum, a man they knew indulged in gratuitous violence was concluded by the Crown Prosecution Service which allowed this animal to walk free.

This pact, which put two men in jail for fifteen years, gave this brute little satisfaction. A year or so later, his decaying corpse was discovered stinking out a filthy squat in Cambridge. Cause of death was determined as a heroin overdose. His fly riddled corpse had laid decomposing there for several weeks before an unbearable stench attracted the attention of the local council. A fitting epitaph for this demonic spirit whose soul was bagged by ambitious cops.

John Hasse suffered from incredible bad luck in his turbulent life. Twice, cohorts had betrayed him in order to save their own scrawny necks and had given Queens evidence against him. Another man of straw, an illiterate peasant spawned in the slums of Liverpool, a repulsive flea infested tramp named Grimes testified against him at a future date resulting in another monumental prison term for this luckless criminal.

His misfortune stemmed from his main flaw the inability to judge the calibre of the miscreants he ran with. An attribute that condemned him to a life behind bars.

CHAPTER 19

Four years had elapsed since the day of the Worcester ambush, four years in which bouts of psychological sword play with penal inquisitors had severely tested my resolve. I was summoned to the wing office by an assistant governor, a schoolboy whelp with a degree in sociology. He called me down to inform me that I was being de-categorised to a category 'B' prisoner. This process made absolutely no difference to my status inside the jail but it affected inter-prison movement whereby I could be transshipped without a posse of gun-toting cops charging alongside and terrorising the community.

"Marvellous, where's the paper hats and balloons?" I quipped reluctant to acknowledge these nonsensical penal theatrics. The naive whelp lacked the intuition to grasp my sarcastic retort.

"Hats and balloons, whatever for?" The academic acorn queried with a puzzled look etched on his immature dial.

"To celebrate your stupidity," I responded as the penny finally dropped and his face turned crimson. I spun around to exit the office leaving the whelp to bathe in his file-filling ritual.

I was experiencing painful problems with the nerves in the traumatised arm. Now that I was deemed to pose no threat to the public, it was decided to send me to an outside hospital for a diagnosis. Bob informed me that I would be going to Birmingham General Hospital in three days' time to see a specialist, his mate had been assigned the task of escorting me accompanied by another Screw. The morning of the appointment a taxi arrived at the prison reception, I was handcuffed to one of the Screws who then sat in the rear of the taxi the other Screw sat in the front with a civilian driver. We exited the gates to merge with traffic and I was surprised to see that no police were present as we hit the road and drove directly to the hospital. To mount an escape with prior knowledge of this procedure would be a simple task with help from outside accomplices prepared to intercept the taxi whereupon the beleaguered officers would be easy prey and more than willing to release me. Force would be the key but the consequences, if captured at this stage of my sentence, were not worth the calculated risk. However, if the opportunity arose for me to abscond without the use of brute force I was prepared to seize the moment.

I arrived at Hospital admissions with my right wrist cuffed to a burly overweight Screw who sweated profusely emitting a foul body odour from his clammy armpits. I was wedged between two officers as I was swept towards a consultation room. A neurologist took a look at the cuffs shackling me to Putrid Armpits and sighed in frustration before indicating to Stench Factor to remove them so he could conduct an inspection of the damage. He refused, stating he had strict security orders that the prisoner must be cuffed at all times. Bob's mate intervened telling the malodorous android to use a bit of common sense and unshackle me.

The programmed buffoon eventually relented muttering to himself as he unlocked the metal bracelets. At this juncture I could have shoved the two Screws out of the way and made a dash for it without much fear of either of them catching me. This thought was bobbing about in my frontal lobe as the consultant poked and probed at my arm. A state of ambivalence gripped me, to go or to stay, the duo of guards totally oblivious to the dilemma I juggled as they both gossiped about playing bingo in the officer's mess. Having concluded the examination the doctor addressed me.

"I have identified a problem with the Median nerve, I believe the problem can be alleviated with an injection that will terminate the function of the nerve. This method may incur some minor side-effects, however the benefits far outweigh any detrimental aspects of this procedure. If you agree, I could arrange for your treatment two weeks from today." He delivered his prognosis in a sing-song tone as if were lecturing to a class of interns. My mind sprang to life, I immediately absorbed the words "two weeks' time," this erased the state of ambivalence coursing through my head - whether to go or stay, I decided to stay and recruit outside aid. The pair of Bingo addicts didn't realise how close they had been to being left twiddling their thumbs wondering where I had fled to.

I dismounted from the examination bed where the perspiring Screw clapped the handcuff onto my right wrist and quickly departed towards the exit, much to the relief of the consultant who was gasping for fresh oxygen in the aftermath of the foul armpit odour that polluted his surgery. Inside the taxi on the way back to the jailhouse, the Asian taxi driver opened the window complaining about the bad smell.

"What the fuck's the stink, man?" He cried, putting his head out of the window to inhale a breath of air. I shifted away from the smelly Screw before replying to the driver.

"It's this dirty lazy fucker. He's in need of a fuckin' bath," I barked out in frustration at the deployment of this filthy human anchor I was shackled to.

"Man, you've got a bad problem," the taxi driver exclaimed shaking his head in disbelief as he continued to pop his head out of the window breathing in deeply.

"It's my glands lads. I'm sorry, it's a medical condition," the sweating stinking blob explained as we all struggled with the foul over-powering scent deposited by him.

"Man, it's bad, I need to get my taxi valeted. Fuck, it's a bad smell." The taxi driver harped on obviously annoyed at carrying a contaminated load. The other escorting officer remained silent, acute embarrassment masking his facial features. Stinkpot wriggled uncomfortably in the seat next to me. I had pulled my t-shirt up to cover my nose and mouth in an attempt to neutralise the potency of the stench.

"You want to get your ass down to the M.O.D. They could utilise your body odour instead of using C.S. Gas. You'll make a fortune," I stated sarcastically to the squirming lump. The Asian driver guffawed loudly.

"Man, the pong is as bad as the shit holes of Calcutta," he blurted as he again popped his head out of the window.

After enduring an hour of discomfort, we eventually arrived back at the prison. I was never so relieved to get back into a jail and breathe in uncontaminated air. The pair of escorts booked me into reception. I turned to the smelly officer and told him that I will refuse to go next time if he is nominated on the escort. He looked at me, his face crimson with discomfort.

I contemplated the trip to the hospital and the opportunity it presented for me to sprint to freedom. I decided to contact a fellow bandit who continued to roam the land plying his lucrative trade and to ask him for a helping hand in securing my flight to freedom. He was a man of honour who cut his own pathway through life's minefields without fear of one person castigating his reputation as a staunch guy. I knew through past experience that he would be quite happy to go the whole hog, hijacking the taxi then plunging the occupants into a living nightmare of sheer terror prior to subduing them. I managed to pass the details of the forthcoming hospital appointment through an intermediary to a friend who would deliver it to the proactive bandit. I carried on as normal mentioning nothing to any of my prison acquaintances about my intentions to fly the coop. I trusted the guy on the outside to have everything sorted including a safe house to stay while I prepared another identity and gathered in some funds.

The day for the chemical injection eventually came to pass, I met Peter, a crippled cat burglar in reception. He had a hospital appointment with a bone specialist because his legs had been smashed to pieces due to a free-fall from a high rise penthouse that he had been in the process of robbing. According to Pete, a skilled mountaineer, the Penthouse was only accessible by scaling the exterior walls. He had penetrated the target's master bedroom wherein he managed to plunder a haul of priceless jewellery. A silent intruder alarm had been triggered alerting trained security guards who burst into the apartment causing Pete to make a desperate bid for freedom. Unfortunately for Pete, as he abseiled down from the roof a guard cut the rope sending Pete crashing to the ground, shattering both of his legs. He struggled to limp along without the aid of crutches. Apparently at Pete's trial he was advised by counsel to throw himself to the mercy of the court, arguing that his injuries prevented him returning to his cat burglary antics. A strong plea of mitigation may persuade the judge to display a morsel of compassion, thus evading a long spell in the slammer. A comical judge accepted the plea, explaining to Pete that he did not have a defensive leg to stand on, however, you are an incorrigible recidivist who has plagued the wealthy people of this country long enough, therefore I am duty bound to make an example of you. You will serve ten years - now hop it.

Pete was relating his tale of woe as we sat sipping coffee in reception. He ranted on about the smug smirk on the judge's face as he tossed in the sarcastic quips. I listened and shook my head by way of sympathetic support for the now disabled mountaineer. I suggested that he should have flung the crutch at the funny bastard. He replied that he would have done only he was wheelchair bound at the time.

I said a silent prayer that I should avoid being shackled to the paraplegic burglar.

A brace of security Screws called me into a cubicle where they frisked me searching for weapons before shepherding me to a waiting prison van where I was cuffed to one of them. Pete hobbled behind me where he too had his wrist chained to a Screw. Instead of the soft target of the taxi, the transport had been upgraded to a prison van with an escort of four officers. A fly in the proverbial ointment of my plan to abscond. I felt like booting the legs off paraplegic Pete. If the opportunity arose I decided to go for broke. I sent word to my pal via prison visits not to produce any weapons at the hospital and wait until he spotted me dashing for the exit where I would expect a car to pick me up. I didn't want an armed breakout which would bring down an army of enforcers and a plethora of negative publicity.

As the van converged on the hospital, I scanned the horizon to familiarise myself with the surrounding terrain, I was also on the alert for comrades in a position to assist my plan. Inside the van, the Screws were debating night shift rotas as we nudged into a parking bay abruptly outside the front entrance. Within seconds of alighting a marked police car pulled in, nestling alongside the prison van, two cops were visible, they remained seated as we disappeared into the Hospital. Cuffed securely to a Screw, I was guided towards admissions with Pete crawling a short distance behind. Mick, a stalwart friend who had turned up, prepared to risk his liberty in order to further my escape, stood in a queue wearing a woollen hat in an attempt to disguise himself. We momentarily locked eyes, he motioned with a balled fist that he was ready and willing to attack the officers; I indicated with my head and mouthed 'Old Bill'; he nodded then rotated his head to absorb the exterior entrance, spotting the parked police vehicle. He remained standing in the queue analysing the situation. Mick was extremely fit, a confident and capable man who would have no problem incapacitating the two Screws assigned to guard me. Once the action erupted, I had total confidence in his ability to accomplish his end of the plot.

A few minutes later I arrived at the consultant's surgery still anchored to the Screw, his accomplice one step ahead of us. The neurologist was fussing about with a syringe the size of a Zulu's spear and he indicated for me to sit on a treatment table. Instead of complying with his command, I remained standing looking disgustedly at the shackles binding me to the Screw.

"Are you taking these fuckin' things off me dickhead?" I snarled, in frustration at the androids fastidious attitude. He glared at me angrily.

"No. I have strict instructions not to remove these cuffs under any circumstances," the obedient mutton-head bleated out, addressing me and the consultant.

Before I could reply the consultant interjected.

"I'm afraid the patient's shirt will have to be removed. I have to insert a needle behind the breastbone. Furthermore I'm not attempting to treat this man while he remains manacled to you," he announced calmly and with an unmistakable air of authority.

The two Screws were momentarily mystified.

"Listen you pair of brain-dead mutants, either you remove these cuffs or take me back to the jail. Pricks." I declared, my adrenalin coursing through my system like stampeding cattle. I was primed up to make a bolt for it in spite of the police patrol car in the vicinity. The moment the mutant unshackled himself I would be gone.

A stalemate situation arose, static tension fused the four

of us together in a motionless time warp as the anchor man contemplated his next move. I had my right fist clenched in readiness to give him a temple shot prior to a dash for the door. I guess his sixth sense relayed a cautionary warning to his decision making process because he suddenly concluded the entire proceedings.

"I'm sorry doctor, but I have my orders. I am returning the inmate back to the jailhouse," he squeaked, his bloated face lighting up bright red.

"Well I never, you dirty cowardly prick. I've a good mind to knock you fuckin' out," I ranted at the human anchor chained to my wrist.

The other Screw panicked thinking I was about to attack his mate and drew his truncheon, the doctor froze petrified at the sudden turn of events.

"Scouse, come on, please behave yourself. My orders are clear. I'm sorry but it's more than my jobs worth to disobey this order. I'm sorry," he whimpered as I dragged him about the room in a fit of rage, his truncheon wielding colleague in tow. A few seconds of scuffling passed, the doctor hot-footed out of his surgery and order was eventually resumed.

I accepted my plot to abscond had been foiled by an obdurate boot-licker who blindly followed orders, I ceased my futile fit of temper, allowing the duo of gladiators to assume control.

An apology was extended to the trembling consultant by the truncheon armed toss-pot as we departed from the scene of the abortive minor surgery. As we approached the Hospital entrance I recognised Mick lurking by a stone pillar waiting to pounce. I gave him the eyes pointing to my cuffs. He was game as they come and he would be with me a hundred percent if I kicked off by attacking the Screw. He mouthed 'Old Bill'. I rapidly computed the shifting dynamics to conclude that the risk factors were not in our favour. A simple dash for freedom could now escalate into a violent struggle, more so with a police patrol car perched in the front. I sighed despairingly, caught Mick's eyes, shrugged my shoulders then shook my head negatively. Mick strolled towards the duo giving them a contemptuous snarl as we sauntered past him.

The fact that a patrol car had coincidently called to the hospital saved the pair of gladiators from losing their detainee. Outside, the patrol car was visible, one cop seated in the passenger seat like Argus. I juggled with the supposition that police presence was either a mere coincidence or there was a breach in my own paranoid security. We boarded the transport, a few brief words were exchanged between the driver and a Screw causing the driver to speed off in the direction of the prison without bothering to wait for paraplegic Pete.

Mick was a dinosaur, the last of a dying breed of outlaws who identified with the culture of a past criminal morality, adhering to a code of practice which embraced a sense of unmitigated loyalty to those that trod alongside him. An abhorrence of authority made it a simple choice for him to pit his will against these upholders of law and order and attempt to spring me. He would have taken as much pleasure as me if the plot had succeeded. He probably drove off in a cloud of depression. We shared a marriage of attitudes that disapproved of collaboration with the law-enforcement stooges. In the past we had conspired, some successfully, some not so successfully, to escape from custodial institutions - both police stations and prisons.

Back in the confines of the calaboose, I was taken straight to the segregation unit and placed on a report. I expected it after the dispute in the consultant's surgery. Unlike the urine-infested squalor of the short-term allocation warehouses, the isolation unit was in pristine condition and manned by decent humans who bore no animosity towards those sinners under their care. I even had access to a radio, newspapers and was offered mugs of tea. I was the only prisoner located there at the time.

At ten a.m. the following day I was mustered before a mock court martial attended by the academic acorn, two guards either side of me as well as the human anchor who had lodged the complaint against me. The baby-faced assistant governor presided over the proceedings with juvenile enthusiasm, brimming with self-importance. He shuffled several papers on a desk in front of him, perused the relevant details of the allegations, shook his juvenile mane then addressed me.

"Smith, you have been charged under section 72 of penal regulations in that you abused and threatened an officer. How do you plead?" he squeaked in a soprano voice. I could not take the college graduate seriously nor the kangaroo court over which he presided.

"Look mate, I can't be bothered playing your silly fuckin' games. Do what your mother told you to do." I made my contempt for this parody of judicial protocol patently obvious. Adjudications never favour the prisoner therefore it's an exercise in futility whilst filling the adjudicator's head with a sense of duty performed. Baby face was stunned by my response, he looked at the Screws for a directive, they too were bemused, I turned to walk back to my isolation cell.

"Smith! Seven days remission and fourteen days segregation," the educated acorn shrieked at my retreating back. I was momentarily restrained by one of the smirking Screws who politely requested I listen to the sanction imposed upon me. I shrugged him off, strolled to the cell and slammed the door behind me. An hour later a note was handed to me with details of the Kangaroo court charade.

Periods of isolation posed no real inconvenience to me,

seclusion enhanced the subconscious into reviving imagery of past, pleasant experiences with family and friends. My mind transcend the bars and claustrophobic walls to cavort freely in the fields of my memory. A holiday away from the chest-beating noise factory.

END OF THE ODYSSEY

Seven years and eight months was endured, staggering through the intestines of a repressive punitive system; it finally came to an end. The gates to freedom opened up to release me back into the natural world of normal gender interaction. It felt as if a titanic boulder had been lifted from my shoulders as I stepped over the threshold of the prison onto the street outside. Gripping a leather sports bag containing a few personal belongings, I paused momentarily inhaled deeply to gather my thoughts then strode forth with a gritty determination. A high powered car pulled up to greet me; I tossed my bag into the back and jumped into the front seat to be whisked away to a new dawn.

In the car, readjusting to the pace of traffic was particularly disturbing and I complained about the speed. My pal laughed at my nervous concerns reassuring me that he was below the speed limit, a factor that previously would not even have registered on my personal radar. I had always driven pacey sports cars with no regard to the legal limits. An updated account of the available opportunities was discussed as we sped towards our destination – Liverpool - and a celebration for surviving the ordeal intact. I felt a surge of elation rushing through my veins as we hit the outskirts of Liverpool, a desire to see my family in tranquil normal settings suddenly embraced me, stirring dormant emotions, an effusion of feelings hitherto repressed flowed throughout my entire body like a fresh water stream. It was an exceptional high that is almost indescribable but familiar to those who have served many years in prison. A resurrection of the soul after years of denial floating in a penal limbo.

I reacquainted myself with the Worcester conspirators who had been at liberty for many years. A party was arranged in a night club to welcome me back to the fold. The coil that linked us together after the fact had somehow dissipated, eroded by a degenerative descent into a world of hedonism, a trip where the partying never ends. I was amazed at the usage of recreational drugs. Cocaine was being snorted as if it were the elixir of life resembling a convention of pharmacists dabbling with each other's products. A total transformation had taken place in the eight years since I graced the nightspots of Liverpool. Gone was the culture of booze and bed; it was booze, drugs, sleepless days fuelled by grams of cocaine allowing the coke-heads to stagger along chattering garbage to each other. Many a good man succumbed to this culture swaying about in a confused smog for months on end until their funds to finance the addiction ran out. The subtle recreational use of coke had spiralled out of control sucking the life's blood from the addict's arteries leaving them penniless, friendless and in some cases homeless. That night was the first time I set eyes on cocaine, Vinnie had been a subscriber to the potent values of coke for a number of years. I questioned his habit and the consequences of his excessive indulgence. His reply became inscribed in my memory forever.

"I can handle it."

He was the essence of a quality man, a good man who had deluded himself by believing he could handle the cancer of cocaine. A self-delusion which ultimately destroyed him, stripping him bare then spitting him out into the gutter. He lost himself, he became a victim of the coke explosion.

New faces had established themselves as forces to be reckoned with, amassing huge sums of money from the narcotics trade. They pranced about in their designer clothes dripping in gold, pockets stuffed with wads of bank notes, blonde trophy pharmaceutical fillies at their elbows. All venues had an abundance of narcotic traders strutting their stuff, publicising their status whilst massaging inflated egos the size of Everest.

Tongues were uncontrollable as they openly bragged about their drug business in front of female pill-popping trophies. The landscape had changed dramatically; drugs had produced a new breed of criminal animal that laboured under the misconception that they were semi-legitimate businessmen. A lack of in-house security measures made the naive traffickers sitting ducks for the enforcement agencies. Survivors used the undercover blueprint invented by the fat Fox to forestall imprisonment by supplying drugs to the addicts whilst supplying information to the police.

A fraudster who had specialised in stolen cheque books, identity duplications, forgery and traveller's cheques approached me at the bar. He was known colloquially as 'The Ferret'.

"Do you want a line?" Was the Ferret's opening gambit, his dilated pupils protruding from their sockets.

I turned to confront the voice in my earhole. I recognised the fraud specialist who appeared to be operating on a different plane to me.

"What the fuck are you talking about?" I naively asked the Ferret who had a silly looking smile on his twisted face.

He proceeded to pull a polythene bag containing half an ounce of cocaine out of his pocket.

"Charlie mate, Columbia's finest marching powder. That's what I'm offering you, Tom," he spluttered incoherently as he attempted to shove the stuff into my hand.

"It's not for me mate." I declined politely out of respect because I'd known the crook for many years. He went on to tell me that he was now dealing coke and earning a steady two to three grand a week. He gossiped about several criminals who had moved into the business, then dropped a bombshell.

"Be careful of Fatso mate, he has been named in dispatches as a grass," he proclaimed, squeezing my forearm as he looked me straight in the eyes. I was taken aback by his statement. I asked him to meet me without alcohol or drugs in his system, enabling us to debate the allegation in slow time.

Before a meeting had been arranged, our conversation was interrupted by the simian featured Fat Sid who slapped me on the back, a broad Judas smile on his face. The Ferret scarpered off faster than an Olympic sprinter vanishing in the blink of an eye.

"Good to see you mate," he lied, offering me bottles of champagne and simultaneously filling my ears with bluster. At this moment his true colours had not been exposed; he was accepted as one of the chaps, a man with connections. Flamboyantly, he pulled out a fistful of fifty pound notes and tossed it on the bar ordering champagne for everyone. A chameleon, a genius at self-preservation. Propositions were made, good times ahead were forecast as the champagne flowed freely and the gang got high. The Ferret never disclosed the finer details of our interrupted conversation and he claimed at a later date that it was the drugs talking, not him. In truth he lost his nerve; moreover the Ferret was wary of any kind of confrontation; the coke had stoked up his bravado, momentarily transforming the pacifist forger into a prize-fighter.

I took time out from the illegal sector of life, disengaging myself from a plethora of fiscal scams that had been put my way. I decided to run parallel with Vinnie who had apparently abandoned his calling as a robber, opting for the entertainment business. He declared there was no value in heavy crime the rewards don't equate with the price of failure. I agreed with his analysis, having suffered and paid that irredeemable price of failure. However my head still retained the cultural norms of prison society straddled with deep anti-establishment beliefs. Beliefs that included conducting your life outside prison as you would inside - meaning you were your own, judge and jury, and punished those who wronged you or your immediate comrades accordingly. Shaking free this penal doctrine wouldn't be easy but if permanent emancipation was to be achieved the psychological bars must be discarded either by adopting a cloak of civilised respectability or emigrating to pastures new.

Several months of freedom raced by; I was still swirling about seeking an ultimate aim and fell into a relationship with the female astrologer. One night I was awoken by a knock on the door; I looked at the time and saw it was two a.m. I slipped into some clothes and proceeded to answer the door. A close friend had dropped by in a state of agitation having just been involved in a confrontation in a club with a known bully. I put my finger to my lips indicating for him to keep his voice down as there were people asleep inside. The upshot was that during the fracas the bully had pulled a blade out and attempted to slash his face, my friend received defensive wounds to his arm during the tussle. He asked me to accompany him to deal with the assailant and I agreed to go with him. Parked outside was a dark coloured car with two men inside. I slid into the rear and the car slowly drove off towards the late night drinking dens of the city centre. The two guys inside were familiar faces I recognised as doormen who worked with my friend; all had been drinking. I was sober as a judge. Alcohol distorts the senses and is a sure fire recipe for disaster when combined with villainy. I regretted embarking on this retributive trip but seeing as I had committed myself, I decided I couldn't allow these intoxicated chest-beaters to lead me down a blind alley into a shit storm.

Aggressive verbal oaths desecrating the family of the knife-man filled the airwaves inside the car as we navigated towards the destination, a seedy unhygienic watering hole that never shut. A place infested with coke-snorting zombies, pill-heads, speed-freaks, sluts looking for a bed and a shower - a low life den of iniquity. Once the culprit had been located he would be blasted in the legs with a shotgun; that was the unanimous decision of the group. Two balaclavas, a pistol and a sawn-down shotgun were in our possession, enough weapons and innate stealth to accomplish the deadly deed. A prevailing unethical perception of the outlaw enveloped me at this time, a code of practise that condoned gross acts of violence as justifiable and righteous. I never gave the consequences a second thought nor the morality of the impending course of action. It was as if we coexisted in a parallel dimension with totally contrasting rules of behaviour.

The neon lit exterior of the drinking den loomed into view; we drove slowly past then looked for a convenient place to park up that was out of sight of the target premises. We all alighted from the car in a dark unlit side street to the rear of the club. One of the doormen headed into the drinking den to ensure the culprit was inside, meantime we prepared ourselves for a rapid assault, checking the firearms and putting the balaclavas over our faces, we were primed and ready to go. Stepping into the shadows we awaited the scouts return; minutes seemed like hours before we heard his footsteps drumming on the pavements of the empty back street. Breathlessly he reported there was no sign of the target or any of his known associates inside the drinking den. Another similar dive was nominated that the knife-man frequented therefore we decided to make haste and check it out.

It began to rain as we pulled on to a main road, driving carefully towards the next location when a police patrol car appeared on our tail. The driver calmly warned us that the 'Old Bill' were following us. He was instructed to keep to the speed limit and not to panic. Let them stop us then we will deal with the situation. Nerves became taut as the patrol car continued to stay behind us, if stopped we had a problem, a problem particularly applicable to me having a deplorable record. It was decided we would disable the police's ability to pursue us by taking their ignition keys and removing the radio transmitter. A set of traffic lights ahead were on red causing us to come to a halt, the patrol car stopped immediately behind us. We were like coiled springs ready to pounce when suddenly the sirens shattered the night air, a blue light started flashing and the car overtook us speeding off in another direction. A huge sigh of relief was shared by all the occupants inside the car, the night's mission was aborted. This incident became a turning point in my life. Reality hit me like a steam engine. I had risked a life sentence because of a drunken fight that had nothing to do with me.

Once I arrived home, I sat alone sipping tea, contemplating the folly of the night's events, it was egotistical stupidity that if adhered to would ultimately lead to disaster. I decided from this day forth all ties to that life style would be curtailed, the elements of gangsterism that remained within my psyche would be purged by treading a different path towards the norms and values of a democratic society. Fate had intervened that night with a warning of the utmost clarity and a sign that intimated to pursue a criminal doctrine would be self-destructive and futureless. An opportunity for redemption was presented to me, to cross over from the twilight zone of crime to enter a dimension with strict guidelines of acceptable behaviour, something which had previously been an alien concept, it had to be seized now or never. Active participation would not become an option, temptation discarded to the trash cans of the past. Fate had convinced me to change direction, a reprogramming of my moral compass, forsaking a code that had dictated how I conducted myself for decades. Such are the quirks of life.

I still kept in touch with some of my old running mates, most had given up the ghost as far as bursting in armed to the teeth. That crime had become as extinct as the dodo. Some drifted into the narcotics trade, most went straight. I still held a sense of camaraderie towards some of these guys because of what we had been through in the past. This bond is felt but never spoken of, an emotional link that couldn't be forged in the virulent drug gangs the haunt the streets today.

A year passed since that awakening during the night of the aborted mission to attack the knife-man, Vinnie plodded on with his leisure business still in cahoots with Fat Sid. Jay had been indicted on several charges of burglary on postal offices. I did my own thing without resorting to prior expertise. Such was the nature of the beast that the gossiping criminal elements kept me abreast of the transactions of those players who ruled the roost in the criminal fields of Liverpool.

Fatso's chameleon reign had long been exposed; he slithered away, secreting himself in pastures new. However his legacy of betrayal had evolved to the extent that it had become pivotal in the state's war against organised crime.

Drugs were the primary source of income for the criminal fraternity attracting a wide spectrum of the social classes. The illiterate slum-dwellers bounced about the streets selling paltry bags of dope to their neighbours, nurturing a capacity for violence to protect their patch and ensure prompt payment from a woeful clientele. Drugs were the currency that determined the behaviour and the status of those wallowing at the bottom of the food chain. The road to freedom was to follow the narcotic route to the wealth and notoriety displayed by the gangsters who had escaped the poverty quagmire by moving to the suburbs.

Most fall into the hands of the authorities and become fodder for penal pissholes; a lifestyle fraught with opiates combined with constipated intellects creating a breed of drifting souls that are easy prey for the cops and their red-robed counterparts. Jail becomes the norm and drug-dealing the sole means of affording a modicum of the capitalist delights - otherwise they dine on scraps and dress in rags.

The indigenous natives who exist in the council ghettoes serve apprenticeships in the drug business. Not for them the skills of employable tradesmen or the minimum wage for whom the poor education process deems them eligible. These communities thrive on the black economy provided by the cultivation of skunk cannabis along with the dispersal of various other powders to the demanding market. Some become pharmaceutical experts by the time they reach their mid-teens. They are capable of gauging the strength of a narcotic by a sniff or dab on an index finger. An Oxford graduate in chemistry would be shamed by the instinctive knowledge of the urban drug-peddler. Horticulturists would be amazed at the farming techniques successfully formulated by the thousands of council estate cannabis cultivators. Every street has farmers growing pot.

The few who are blessed with cunning and logistical skills graduate from street-dealing to importation and trafficking narcotics within a clandestine web of outlets. The market is well established and firmly entrenched across the whole of the U.K., demand exceeds supply. Cokeheads can be observed snorting their brains away within the boundaries of royal palaces, high state office, most police stations, and every night club in the country. Cocaine is endemic, a pandemic which generates billions of pounds globally.

Narcotics seduce the senses, erode away the reins of common decency and instil a wanton greed. Consequences become irrelevant to the trafficker who has engaged in the narcotic trade over a sustained period of time. Complacency, an arch nemesis of criminality can often envelop the felon in a cloak of invincibility that creates the illusion that he is providing a service to the community and a belief that he is a legitimate entrepreneur. This delusionary trait may ultimately seal his fate as guards drop and wealth is openly flaunted creating a blip upon the police radar.

Modern day surveillance technology is so advanced that any criminal that appears upon the radar system is doomed. The lawbreaker can be considered to be in pre-arrest mode and a candidate for the jailhouse. It is an irrefutable fact that only a fool would misconstrue - if one operates as an active criminal in the field of narcotics whilst under police observation, then that felon is volunteering to join the wretched ranks of the ever-increasing penal population. A wounded and bloodied lamb has more chance of escaping from a pack of ravenous wolves than a renowned drug trafficker has of eluding capture.

Some, however, do avoid the pitfalls of their chosen and somewhat precarious profession. These exceptions to the rule are invariably at the hub of organised crime; many amass fortunes; they are more or less connected to every strata of the importation and distribution of narcotics; these drug barons survive with the blessing of guardian angels. They have entered into a Faustian pact with the law enforcers who sanction and condone all the illicit activities of the baron. In exchange for immunity from prosecution, a pledge is taken to betray fellow dealers and provide the necessary information to secure a conviction, preferably with the unsuspecting comrade ambushed red-handed. They, in essence, enrol as plain clothes policemen, gathering intelligence against drug operations whilst being instrumental in plotting the downfall of their cohorts.

The chosen few have been identified and selected by the authorities as potential undercover operators because of the status and adulation held by those at the vanguard of the drug industry. Furthermore, the potential quisling must be glib tongued, politically astute with as many faces as a town hall clock. Satisfied that the candidate's profile compliments police criteria, the die is cast, and the unwary target is swooped upon and covertly shuffled off for intense interrogation and grooming sessions.

Dossiers are produced depicting the target as an integral part of incriminating conspiracies; moreover, indisputable evidence involving the suspect in major drug importations will be placed in the mix. Testimony exacted from indicted felons which implicates the battered soul as a major source in the drug supply chain is used to crush any wavering spirits. He is now firmly nailed to the cross.

Confronted by an unassailable mountain of evidence, a realisation seeps into his mind-set that options are severely restricted. In fact, if he retains a gossamer thread of honour, he is accepting that he is doomed and about to be mummified courtesy of the penal system. The advent of "The Proceeds of Crime Act" increases the mental torpor due to the two-tier punishment construed to deprive the accused of all assets as well as a monumental fine that is impossible to pay.

The civil servant who invoked this unjust Act has eradicated the "risk reward" ethos previously adopted by major criminals. The risk now far outweighs the reward because of the stripping of assets and confiscation of all accessible possessions which leaves the suspect and his kith and kin denuded except for the blood that runs through their illicit veins.

The ensuing fine plus the subsequent double figure sentence for failure to comply with these draconian fiscal demands tests the will and ethical code of the sternest of men. A person crazy or brave enough to attempt to comply with the Crown's punitive fiscal defilement levied against them will ultimately be indicted for money laundering and subsequently become immersed in a legal miasma with no escape.

Floundering in a pit of despair, a high ranking enforcer offers the offender a trade, a trade that allows him his freedom; a man of honour would shun this bartering cop and accept the consequences of his past misdemeanours. Men of honour are the exception - it would be easier to find a jihadist quoting from the bible than to witness a trafficker exhibiting a sliver of loyalty. Prison accommodates the few honourable criminals that pursued the narcotic paths. These naive convicts were probably sacrificed by an undercover comrade who capitulated in order to preserve his own skin and to continue living an extravagant lifestyle.

THE FAUSTIAN TRADE

Facing decades devoid of the sweet fruits of freedom and almost certain financial ruin, self-preservation prevails and an agreement is reached. The bright light of liberty banishes the suffocating blanket of despair as the felon embarks on a journey of treachery by becoming a fully-fledged intelligence agent. His soul has been bought.

The new recruit is designated a code name and twenty-four hour access to his handler. A script writer, specialising in cover-ups is assigned to ensure the recruit remains above suspicion after pawning comrades captured in the process of trafficking caches of narcotics. Fictionalised scenarios abound echoing across all criminal airwaves after each coup, exonerating the shark's perfidy and casting doubt about the bona fides of others involved in the plot.

Depending upon the potency and influence wielded by the subject of this sordid act of immorality, a host of economic inducements come into play. Assuming the man is benefitting from a lifestyle of opulence provided by drug operations, his handlers will facilitate a contract allowing him to retain ownership of properties and maintain a luxurious routine. Furthermore, if the pact yields positive results culminating in major convictions and drug seizures, the tout becomes eligible for fiscal rewards. The bigger the contraband seized the bigger the prize given to the tout.

If sustained over a period of time the subject gravitates towards legitimacy aided by cop cohorts whose protective umbrella brings on board the Inland Revenue and The Home Office. On the backs of his brothers, and untold misery inflicted upon those unfortunates entombed whilst under the tout's sphere of influence, he strides forth blessed by law enforcement agencies in conjunction with the power of the State.

The ex-cop, who unmasked Fatso, also denounced notorious villains who had succumbed to police inquisition and joined the elitist ranks of blessed informants. A particular quisling was awarded four-hundred thousand after one high profile operation brought about the downfall of a multi-million pound crime syndicate. He was a prime mover in a cocaine conspiracy but failed to get mentioned in arrest dispatches due to the skills of his cop scriptwriter. His ill-fated companions are decomposing within the bowels of the penal pissholes. They are painfully unaware that this specimen was responsible for the collapse of their criminal empire along with the confiscation of millions of pounds in currency and assets. Apparently, he continues to communicate with the sacrificial lambs, even having the temerity to send money and drugs into the jails to ease their burden whilst simultaneously enhancing his reputation as a stand-up guy.

One particular member of this exclusive club of Quislings displayed the flamboyancy and panache of a leading Hollywood star. He strutted like a V.I.P. exuding confidence, portraying himself as business tycoon, flaunting his wealth at civic functions, charity shin-digs and major sporting events. This guy would be at the forefront of any entertainment festival that attracted celebrities. Such was his aptitude for his role as an informant that he coordinated arrest and discovery procedure. He boldly reprimanded his police handlers if intelligence provided failed to result in a successful indictment. He deserved an Oscar for his acting abilities.

Only those well-versed in the machinations of the tangled labyrinths of the international narcotic trade are poached then presented with a jail-free card. They are encouraged to continue, uninterrupted, plying their trade simultaneously digging penal graves in which to bury unsuspecting allies. Devoid of a conscience, the sheer gusto for the act of betrayal emitted by a jail-free card carrying quisling astonished the cops. He voluntary travelled incognito to South America to liaise with the C.I.A., providing intelligence as if he were an espionage agent negotiating on behalf of the British government. A copy of a memo appropriated by a thief gave details of an undercover quisling's crusade against organised crime.

Internal Memo,

Informant X, code name, Barracuda.
Subject remains the most effective ammunition in this force's armoury in the fight against organised crime. Ten years have elapsed since the policy was introduced and exceeded all expectations. Barracuda has been responsible for the seizure of narcotics with a street value of a billion pounds.
Intelligence provided by him has resulted in the arrest and imprisonment of some one-hundred hard-core drug traffickers. Sophisticated international cartels have been exposed and nullified due to intelligence supplied by the subject.
It is of paramount importance to protect his identity and to ward off any suspicion of his much-valued intelligence work. To ensure this anonymity, heads of national crime agencies are to terminate any past and future investigations concerning Barracuda.
Implementation of this strategy was approved and sanctioned at ministerial level.

Signed,

Crime Commissionaire
Richard Head,

Along with other documentation pilfered was operational data identifying other counterintelligence recruits eligible for the platinum jail-free pardon. The grapevine became volcanic after this secret filtered into criminal conduits. Panic and paranoia prevailed sparking an exodus of proactive traffickers disappearing with their booty.

Rumours sprouted about the fleeing mob spotted congregating at seedy late night Spanish drinking dens dancing the legs off themselves. Incapable of tip-toeing through the shadows, most of the runaways were subsequently captured and tossed into the slammer. A hypothesis can be formulated from this analysis that contemplating a career as drug smuggler is the equivalent of volunteering to be suicide bomber. Public health warnings should be issued by the police to aspiring rooky dope pushers.

Since the introduction of platinum-licensed felon, the jailhouse population has doubled to a figure in excess of eighty thousand. The vast majority incarcerated for drug related offences. The U.K. jail more offenders per-capita than any other country on the planet except for the corrosive U.S.A. - the Yanks philosophy is "if it's black, semi-literate and speaks, jail it."

The jailhouses are crammed, the dope dealing flourishes hydra-headed. Entomb a quartet of traffickers and before the cell door has slammed, five more will have replaced the fallen felons. "More jails," clamour the politicians, making it one of the fastest growing industries in the country. Eventually the ghettoes will be ring-fenced making them virtual open penal camps with those inside tagged, processed and requiring a pass for exit periods.

For those dope-fiends stalking the council estate corridors, take heed; there is no escaping the unethical sword wielded by the law enforcers. They hold all the cards utilising the law and a morally defunct judiciary to crush any who refuse to genuflect at the altar of capitalist conformity.

The future is grim for those enticed by dreams of wealth afforded by a career in the narcotics trade. A minefield of adverse tribulations waits in ambush. To deal you have to trust more than one person, therein lies the fragility of the business. To bestow trust places a person in a position of vulnerability as the trustee may be a tout and engineer an arrest. A man has more chance of survival selling copies of the bible to Islamic extremists in Syria than a grafter has in the narcotics game.

Tom Smith

YOUR BEST FRIEND MAY BE YOUR WORST ENEMY

THE MOBILE PHONE

Solving crime has been made considerably easier for law enforcers since the innovation of the mobile phone. It is a tracking device mapping geographical movements of the phone holder whilst recording all business and social contacts. The mobile phone is an accessible endemic communicational log book that bounces about in cyber space available to the numerous agencies who wish to pry into the activities of a phone holder. It is an essential piece of equipment for narcotic traders that links supply chains to consumers leaving indelible digital fingerprints. This overt digital forensic data emanating from the lethargic lips of drug traders may prove to be instrumental in sealing a criminal conviction.

Crime crews opt for the pay-as-you-go phones, chopping and changing them frequently in the belief it confuses surveillance operators. A fallacy held by indolent buffoons lacking the mental capacity to understand the penal hole they are digging themselves into. One trafficking genius was known to parade like a peacock throughout urban drug conduits juggling with six mobile phones. The authorities had a field day with the information gleaned from this paragon of stupidity. A cop compared him to a performing seal publically proclaiming his chosen profession; all the retard lacked was fluorescent jacket advertising cocaine for sale.

Conversing over cyber airwaves is akin to speaking on the radio. If the speaker is of interest to the State or subordinate agencies they tune in, listen, and if the snippets of chitchat are incriminating they record. Intelligence is voluntarily shoved down the cop's flappy lugholes via a daily torrent of cyber drug gossip. The criminal who conducts his illicit trade down the mouthpiece of a mobile gadget not only jeopardises his own freedom but the security status of any person foolish enough to engage in cyber verbals with him. Conspiracy laws are heavily loaded in favour of the Crown, the reverse burden of proof suffices in all drug related cases; a mere telephone conversation with an indicted felon can end with a lengthy spell behind bars. Innocence or guilt is immaterial; proof that a phone number linking any person to a known trafficker is enough for the paranoid and ruthless police piranhas to condemn the ill-fated soul to life in the calaboose.

Many an innocent man is decomposing in some penal pisshole for socialising with drug traders, unaware at the time of the nature of the felon's trade. This is a recurring phenomenon among those natives marginalised by birth and who squat in drab housing estates. Judicial Process deems these unfortunates guilty of whatever indictment the Crown conjures up against them. A prejudicial cancer plagues the legal system whereby the onus is on the individual to disprove the case against them. The red-robed rabble posture like wise old owls administering unpalatable jail terms to defendants whose only crime is to possess a mobile phone that received a call from a trafficker. Using legal semantics they validate persecution of slum dwellers and the swarms of poorly educated suspects that litter the courthouses quoting medieval laws draped in out dated guff. If Mother Theresa and the Pope swore a defendant was sipping wine with them in the Vatican it would have little impact in staving off a conviction. If you are born poor, dress like a scarecrow, barely literate, low aspirations and possess a mobile phone then watch out if you fall foul of the law. Chances are that you will end up roaming penal cell blocks for the remainder of your days bemoaning the injustice induced by being bred on the wrong side of the street.

Printed in Great Britain
by Amazon